Made in Michigan: Tales & Recipes

By Carole Eberly

Cover & Illustrations by Kathi Terry

Copyright 2002
Eberly Press
403 Frankfort Avenue
Elberta, Michigan 49628
michigancooking.com

ISBN 978-0-932296-16-0

Introduction

Made in Michigan: Tales & Recipes began in 1994 when the editor of a wonderful city magazine, Lansing City Limits, asked me to be a food columnist. While I love to cook and have written 14 other cookbooks, I also love to write. . . about anything. These essays are from, or inspired by, the columns I wrote for that magazine for five years. Almost all are about life in Michigan; others are about this Michigander's travels around the globe.

You'll find chapters for every month on your calendar. The recipes feature dishes that go along with the essays.

Have fun reading and cooking!

Carole

Tales and recipes to enjoy....

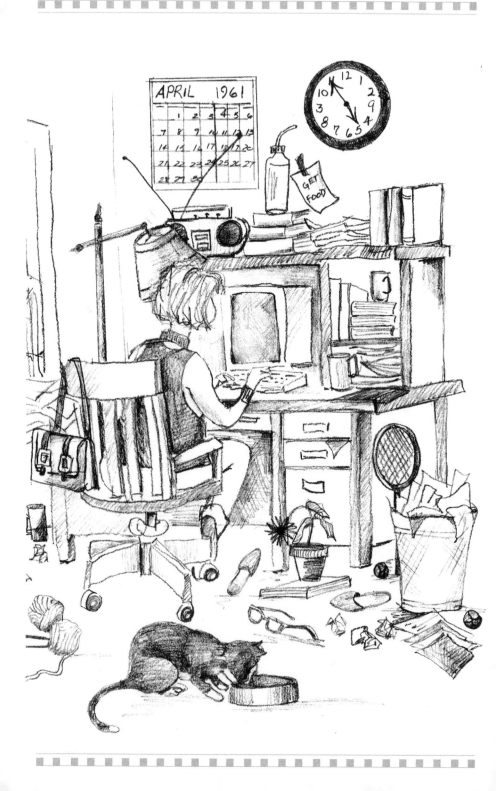

Chaos is my friend

I ran across three magazines in the beauty shop this week that featured pieces on how to start a new life this year. They told me how to organize my home/ office/ life. They promised everything from a salary hike to clearer skin if I would just dump those boxes of cancelled checks from 1968.

Well, why do this? Why is it that neatniks want to change the nesters? Why are we the ones made to feel guilty?

Recently a colleague stood at my office door and peered in. "I can only work on one thing at a time," she said, surveying the piles of papers, books and computer disks on my desk. "Me too," I agreed as I graded papers in my lap. She disappeared, only to return five minutes later. "I find it easier to work when my desk is clean," she proclaimed. "Good," I offered.

Surmising that I hadn't gotten the point, she took a deep breath and blasted, "You know, a cluttered desk can lead to a cluttered mind." Rather than hand her a bottle of Mr. Clean and a rag, I answered, "Could be." Obviously she hadn't read the sticker on my file cabinet which read: "Organized people are just too lazy to look for things."

Why we comfortable nesters bother organized people so much has always puzzled me. I don't care if anyone wants to run around with a spray can of Lysol and colored file folders. And yet I run into people who insist on changing my lifestyle. I had a roommate in college who was so obsessed with neatness that she would remake my bed in the morning so the stripes in our plaid bedspreads lined up together – even though the beds were four feet apart. My desk was such an affront to her eyes that she bought a rattan screen to block the view. She went on to cheerfully marry a man who insisted she iron his underwear.

We, of the comfort zone, are the ones who can be counted on to retrieve anything. It may take a while, but we have it all. Need a playbill from "The Sound of Music" in 1973? The address of the Athens Gate Hotel? The names of the astronauts on all the Challenger missions? Give us a call. We're the historians of the universe. Yeah, we know about libraries and Yahoo, but deep down we really don't trust these things to keep the important documents needed for civilization to continue. Things like Chinese placemats, baby teeth, Easter basket grass from 1987.

My friend Willah, another historian, recently sent me an empty 1982 baking powder can because she knows I like to cook. What a wonderful present. It could come in handy someday for . . . .

We collectors are a generous sort, sharing our booty with the helplessly organized. People always hit me up for gumballs, matches, Kleenex, toothpicks, loose change, index cards and pens – all things I carry in my coat pocket.

My purse is a miniature version of my house. Last winter a woman in the Meijer's parking lot could not get into her car because the lock was frozen. I simply extracted a giant bottle of de-icer from my purse. Problem solved. We are prepared.

The interior of her car, by the way, was spotless. Right now, in my backseat I have – among other things – a roaster from last Thanksgiving with three shoes in it, a fireplace poker and a five-pack of Vernor's bought last year sometime. I could find a use for each of those items given the proper circumstance.

Think. How many times have you heard the saying: "As soon as I throw it out, I know I will need it. " Well, we don't have that problem. And...we're not obsessed by the need to change neatfreaks. They can just do their crazy little "everything in it's place" routine. Doesn't bother us a bit. We're too busy having fun collecting more stuff for our nests.

Think I'll write an article: "Become a Pack Rat; Watch Your Wallet Grow. " It makes as much sense to me as getting rich by being organized. I once saw Thomas Edison's work desk – it was a mess. And, he ended up rich. He probably had clear skin, too.

I believe this whole neatnik thing is a scam to keep people busy and their minds off really important things. Like anthrax or the IRS or baking brownies.

Brownies?
Did you say brownies?

Or course, you know never to over-bake brownies – much better to underbake so they're chewy...and messy.

Miniature Brownies

*(You can eat more of these for fewer calories –
or something like that.)*

Nut crust:
3 tablespoons butter
3 tablespoons sugar
3/4 cup finely chopped walnuts

Blend butter with sugar and chopped nuts.   Line 9-inch
square pan with foil and press nut mixture over bottom of
pan.

Brownie filling:
1/2 cup butter
1 cup sugar
3 eggs
2 squares unsweetened chocolate, melted
1 teaspoon vanilla
1/3 cup all purpose flour, sifted
1/2 teaspoon baking powder
1/8 teaspoon salt

Place all ingredients in mixing bowl.   Mix at low speed
until smooth.   Turn into nut-lined pan and bake at 325
degrees 35-40 minutes.   Cool.

Chocolate glaze:
1/2 cup semi-sweet chocolate chips
2 tablespoons butter

Melt chocolate; add butter and stir
until smooth.   Pour over cooled brownies.
 Put in refrigerator to cool.
Cut into mini-pieces.

Polka Dot Brownies

1/2 cup shortening
2 squares unsweetened chocolate
3/4 cup flour
1/2 teaspoon baking powder
1/2 teaspoon salt
2 eggs
1 cup sugar
1 teaspoon vanilla
1/2 cup nuts, chopped
1/2 cup miniature marshmallows

Melt shortening and chocolate over hot water. Cool. Sift
flour with baking powder and salt. Beat eggs in a large
bowl until light. Add sugar, then the chocolate mixture.
Blend. Add flour mixture, vanilla, nuts and
marshmallows. Mix well. Bake in greased 8-inch square
pan at 350 degrees for 30-35 minutes.

Hershey Syrup Brownies

(Use the regular size can of chocolate syrup – not the 10-gallon one. Of course, you could always find something to do with the 9-plus gallons left over.)

1 stick butter
1 cup sugar
4 eggs
1 teaspoon vanilla
1 cup flour
1 can Hershey chocolate syrup
1/2 cup chopped nuts

Mix the butter and sugar well. Mix in eggs and vanilla. Add flour, syrup and nuts. Pour into a 13x9-inch cake pan. Bake at 350 degrees for 40-45 minutes. Cool. Spread with Easy Fudge Frosting.

Easy Fudge Frosting

6 tablespoons butter
6 tablespoons milk
1-1/2 cup sugar

Bring ingredients to a rolling boil, beating vigorously. Beat and boil for just 30 seconds. Add 1/2 cup chocolate chips and beat until it reaches spreading consistency.

Marshmallow Brownies

(Do not make before trying on bathing suits.)

2 sticks butter
1/2 cup cocoa
4 eggs
2 cups sugar
2 teaspoons vanilla
1/2 teaspoon salt
1-1/2 cups flour
3/4 of a 13-oz. jar of marshmallow crème

In small saucepan, melt the butter and cocoa together. In larger bowl, blend eggs, sugar and vanilla. Add flour, salt and the cocoa mixture. Mix about 2 minutes (just until blended). Spread into a greased 13x9-inch pan. (Mixture will be thick.) Bake for 20-25 minutes at 350 degrees. While hot, spoon, at random, the marshmallow crème. Let sit about 2 minutes before spreading – needs to melt a bit. Then gently spread over the brownies. Let cool completely before topping with the frosting. (It is not a pretty sight at this point, but who cares?)

Frosting

1/4 cup cocoa
3/4 stick melted butter
2 1/2 cups powered sugar
1 tablespoon milk

Mix until creamy.
Spread gently on top of
marshmallow topping.
Cut and serve after
an hour (ha!).

Applesauce Brownies

2 squares unsweetened chocolate
1/2 cup butter
1 cup packed brown sugar
1/2 cup applesauce
2 eggs
1 teaspoon vanilla
1-1/3 cups Bisquick
1/4 teaspoon baking soda
1/2 cup chopped nuts

Heat chocolate and butter in a saucepan over low heat, stirring constantly, until melted. Remove from heat and cool. Mix in brown sugar, applesauce, eggs and vanilla. Stir in Bisquick and baking soda. Spread in 13x9-inch greased pan. Sprinkle with nuts. Bake at 350 degrees for about 25-30 minutes. Cool. Cut into 1 1/2-inch squares.

Peanut Butter Brownies

(One more reason to keep peanut butter on hand.)

1 cup peanut butter
1/2 cup butter, softened
2 cups brown sugar
3 eggs
1 teaspoon vanilla
1 cup flour, sifted
1/4 teaspoon salt

Beat peanut butter, butter and
sugar in a bowl until creamy.
Mix in eggs and vanilla.
Add in flour and salt, mixing
well.   Spread in greased
13x9-inch pan.   Bake at
350 degrees for 30-35
minutes.

Mick Jagger and me

(I wrote a version of this column for the Lansing City Limits' first edition in 1994. At that time the city was all cranked up for the Rolling Stones' appearance at Spartan Stadium. I was asked to write something about Mick Jagger. Here are the results. I also had to include this because, as you all know, the British flag once flew over Michigan.)

It would be great to relate a personal story about Mick Jagger. But truth is the closest we ever came to sharing anything was probably our reading of the same stories in the British tabloids – the ones with headlines like "Adolf Hitler was a Woman," "Clintons Adopt Alien Baby" and, of course, "Killer Bug Ate My Face."

I, like so many other professors from MSU, taught summer courses in Britain. Since my area was journalism, it was with great gusto I read their thirteen daily newspapers. And I could read this mountain of newsprint with impunity under the guise of research or soaking up local culture. Sundays were bonanzas with inserts, magazines and special editions. I bought them all, including the "Sunday Sport," a paper that peddlers hid in brown paper bags by their feet. Being chastised more than once for requesting the Sport was a sport in itself. "A lady like you should not be reading (interpret as looking at, words were unnecessary) such unsavory material." But, hey, this was London. Fork it over – unsavory stuff and all. Killer newsstands routinely ate my ten pound notes.

Then it was off to Hyde Park to spread out my purchases while listening to some Communist, Druid or Jehovah's Witness get pounded by passersby at Speaker's Corner. A favorite column of mine listed the schedules of the royals. You know,

Queen:
· luncheon with Queen Beatrix, 11:30 a. m. ,
  Buckingham Palace
· tea party, Kew Gardens, 4 p. m.
· wave to the unwashed,
  Covent Garden Opera House steps, 8 p. m.

Although I dogged the heels of various royals from time to time, I never did have a conversation with the queen. However, I once stayed down the road from her in Scotland when she was at the Palace of Holyroodhouse. I encamped at the Waverly Hotel in downtown Edinburgh where I shared a bathroom with her bodyguards. (I thought it a bit strange that her bodyguards were not with her body and, also, that while she probably had dozens of bathrooms at the palace they had to share mine. Oh well.) I said good morning to one of her protectors as he emerged and I waited outside the bathroom, towel in hand, for the shower. He nodded. I asked how the queen was doing, but he just slammed the door to his room. I looked around for any doubloons that might have slipped out of his pocket without success.

Later that day I saw him hold the door for the queen as she entered Jenners Department Store. I wanted to suggest he at least ask for a room with a private bath at contract renewal time. But local Scots, who were less than enamored with the royal family, said he deserved his fate. So I went over to Rose Street and quaffed a brew instead.

But, back to Mick. I haven't researched what he eats, but I do know it's not enough. Perhaps he could use some of the following recipes to bulk up a bit. These are collected from a variety of sources in Britain. I have Americanized them, using our weights and measures as well as short-cut ingredients. They are some of my favorites from the Isle of Wight, Cambridge, London, St. Andrews, Aberdeen and around.

Syllabub

(In the sixteenth century, syllabub was made by milking a cow into a bowl of ale or cider. However, since most of us don't have cows in our garages, follow these instructions instead for a tasty dessert.)

2 cups chilled whipping cream
3 ounces sherry
1-1/2 ounces brandy
1/4 cup sugar
Juice of half a lemon
Grated nutmeg

Combine all ingredients in a chilled bowl and beat until thick. Pour into wine glasses and chill.

Mushroom Appetizer

16 large sliced mushrooms
4 slices chopped bacon
1/2 cup whipping cream
1/2 cup white wine
4 tablespoons grated cheese

Sauté the mushrooms with bacon. Divide into four individual ramekin dishes. Beat cream until stiff; beat in wine. Spoon over top of mushrooms. Top with cheese and broil until cheese is crisp and golden.

Apricot and Coconut Balls

1 cup chopped dried apricots
1/4 cup brown sugar
1 cup sweetened condensed milk
1/4 cup coconut

Mix apricots, sugar and condensed milk together.   Chill until firm, about one hour.   Form into balls and roll in coconut. Refrigerate or freeze until serving.

Ginger and Walnut Tea Bread

(If you're a real ginger lover, you can put in two teaspoons of ground ginger.   Wonderful with afternoon tea.)

1/2 cup sugar
1/2 cup shortening
1 egg
1/2 cup dark molasses
1-1/2 cups flour
3/4 teaspoon salt
3/4 teaspoon baking soda
1 teaspoon ginger
1/2 cup boiling water
3 tablespoons minced candied ginger
1/2 cup chopped walnuts

Cream sugar and shortening until light and fluffy.   Beat in egg and molasses.   In a separate bowl, sift dry ingredients.   Mix well.   Stir into shortening mixture alternately with boiling water. Stir in candied ginger and walnuts.   Pour into a greased 8x8-inch pan and bake at 350 degrees for 35-40 minutes.

Basic Scones

(A must with afternoon tea. Serve split and lathered with the thickest whipped cream — clotted cream is used in Britain — you can find and strawberry jam. If you want, you can add 1/3 cup raisins to make fruit scones.)

2 cups self- rising flour	1 teaspoon baking powder
Pinch of salt	4 tablespoons butter
3 tablespoons sugar	Milk

Sift flour, baking powder and salt into a bowl. Rub in butter until mixture resembles coarse breadcrumbs, then stir in sugar. Mix with enough milk to make a soft, light dough. Roll out dough on floured surface to about 1- inch thickness; cut into 2- inch rounds. Place on ungreased baking sheet and brush with milk or beaten egg. Bake at 450 degrees for 10- 12 minutes until just golden brown. Wrap in a tea towel immediately after baking so scones remain soft.

Chicken and Shrimp

4 boneless chicken breasts	1/4 cup butter
1/2 cup chopped almonds	1/2 cup shelled shrimp
4 tablespoons sherry	1/2 cup cream

Pound chicken breasts flat.
Sauté lightly in butter. Add almonds and shrimp; cook for 3- 4 minutes, until shrimp is pink and done. Pour in sherry and cream; stir and simmer (don't boil) a few minutes until sauce thickens.

Pork and Sherry

6 pork cutlets
1/2 cup flour
1/4 cup butter
2 cups canned button mushrooms
1/2 cup sherry
1-1/2 cups cream

Shake cutlets with flour in a paper bag. Sauté in butter until tender. Remove to serving platter and keep warm. Heat mushrooms with sherry in pan. Turn heat to low and stir in cream; simmer (make sure it doesn't boil) until sauce thickens. Pour over cutlets.

Lemon Curd

(Like eating a lemon meringue pie without the meringue and crust. Use as a spread on toast or scones. Can also be eaten with a spoon standing over the sink.)

1 cup sugar
1/4 cup butter
Rind and juice of two lemons
2 eggs

In the top of a double boiler stir sugar, butter, rind and juice over high heat until sugar melts. Reduce heat to medium. Beat eggs in small bowl. Stir small amount of hot mixture into eggs; pour eggs into lemon mixture. Stir constantly until it thickens. Pour into a jar and chill.

Oatcakes

(These are crunchy crackers. Serve with cheese, a dip or spread with butter – or just eat.)

1/2 cup flour
2 cups finely ground oatmeal
Pinch of salt
2 tablespoons melted shortening
Boiling water

Mix together the flour, oatmeal and salt in a bowl. Stir in shortening and add just enough boiling water to make a stiff dough. Roll out dough very thin on a board covered with ground oatmeal. Cut into triangles or 3-inch rounds. Place on greased baking sheets and bake at 350 degrees for 25-30 minutes.

Potted Cheshire Cheese

(You can use cheddar cheese in the recipe. If the cheese is starting to go, just scrape the mold off and – voila – you've got another week or so of shelf life. Eat sliced with walnuts and pears at the end of dinner.)

8 oz. Cheshire cheese
2-3 tablespoons unsalted butter
2 tablespoons sherry
1 teaspoon mace

Grate cheese finely and mix with softened butter. Add the sherry and mace; mix well. Press well down in a pot. Chill.

Finger pickin' good

There's this thing with five strings and a neck sitting on my dining room table, daring me to pick it up. It's called a banjo. I bought it, along with a well-worn case, three finger picks and a video entitled "Beginner's Banjo Video: Volume 1", after shopping for 15 minutes at Elderly Instruments. According to the video, I should be playing such well-known tunes as "Banjo in the Hollow," "Cumberland Gap," and "Foggy Mountain Breakdown" in two weeks. Murphy Henry, my video teacher, said the first thing I needed to do to play the banjo was to get a banjo. So far, so good. But my banjo also came with an acoustical setup so I can annoy neighbors and passersby as I make my ascent to the pinnacle of banjoism.

Taking the banjo plunge was only a matter of time. From the Mummers to Dolly Parton to Steve Martin, banjo players seem to have more fun than people who play other instruments. (I've never seen a harpist with an arrow through the head.) In high school, people played the clarinet, trumpet or tuba because there wasn't much of a call for banjos in the marching band. Now that I don't have to worry about music credits anymore, it's time to play what I want.

I wasn't really sold, though, until a banjo got me out of a speeding ticket. A hippie friend of mine - complete with love beads and beat-up sandals - picked, strummed and wailed away as I drove through the Upper Peninula. I wasn't watching the speedometer, but a state trooper was.

A glance in the rear view mirror confirmed those were lights flashing behind me. Like all heavy pedal miscreants, I optimistically thought he was after someone else. But there he was, two feet from my rear bumper. I pulled over as vanloads of kids laughed, pointed and sped on.

After the usual driver's license-proof of insurance stuff, the trooper eyed my banjo-buddy, still mindlessly picking away, oblivious to the mundane world of the $100 fine. The trooper leaned into the car. "How well do you play that thing?" he inquired. Banjo buddy tightened a few strings, loosened a couple of others. Frizzy blonde hair flailed in all directions, eyes stared into another galaxy. Then something like a jazzed up version of "Turkey in the Straw" poured in, around and out of the car. A performance worthy of Carnegie Hall - well, a barn in Tennessee, anyway. The trooper smiled, handed me my license and said, "Slow down and enjoy Michigan." You bet!

I now have grand plans to form my own group consisting of me, a bagpiper, an underemployed washboardist, and a student flutist. We could either sound real Celtic - or real bad. But first I've got to pop in this video. Everyone needs a hobby.

And now for some banjo-pickin' food - stuff that will stick with you during these cold days.

Cheddar Cheese Chowder

(Won't help me get into my size 8. But, what the heck, neither will any of these other recipes. I'll diet for sure in the spring.)

3 cups water
4 chicken bouillon cubes
4 medium peeled and diced potatoes
1 medium chopped onion
1/2 bunch chopped broccoli
1/2 cup diced green pepper
1/2 pound sliced mushrooms
1/3 cup butter
1/3 cup flour
3 1/2 cups milk
4 cups shredded sharp cheddar cheese

Bring water and bouillon cubes to a boil in large pot. Add vegetables and simmer until tender. Melt butter in heavy saucepan; stir in flour and cook 1 minute. Gradually add milk. Cook over low heat until thickened, stirring constantly. Add cheese, stirring until melted. Stir cheese sauce into vegetable mixture. Cook until heated. Do not boil. Serves 8.

Bacon and Potato Chowder

(You can add 3 8-ounce cans of minced clams, if you like. Use the clam liquid to make up part of the 4 cups water.)

1/2-pound sliced bacon
2 medium sliced onions
2 tablespoons flour
4 cups water
5 large peeled and diced potatoes (about 5 cups)
2 teaspoons salt
1/4 teaspoon pepper
4 cups milk
1 cup half and half
2 tablespoons butter

Brown bacon in large pot. Add onion and cook until tender, about 5 minutes. Stir in flour until well blended. Slowly add water to pot, stirring until thickened. Add potatoes, salt and pepper. Cover and cook until potatoes are tender, about 10 minutes. Stir in milk, cream and butter. Cook until heated through but do not boil. Mash a few of the potato chunks to thickened chowder, if desired.
Serves 12.

Seafood Gumbo

(Shrimp and crabmeat together - yum!)

3/4 cup flour
3/4 cup oil
2 cups chopped onion
1 cup chopped celery
1 cup chopped green pepper
2 cloves crushed garlic
1 1-pound can crushed tomatoes
1 bay leaf
1 tablespoon salt
1 teaspoon thyme
1/2 teaspoon pepper
2 tablespoons Worcestershire sauce
1/2 teaspoon Tabasco (or to taste)
8 cups water
1 pound medium shelled shrimp
1 pound crabmeat

In a large pot, stir flour and oil until blended over low heat. Cook, stirring often, about 30 minutes or until mixture is dark brown. Stir in onion, celery, green pepper and garlic. Cook 10 minutes. Add tomatoes, bay leaf, salt, thyme, pepper, Worcestershire and Tabasco. Cook 30 minutes. Add water and bring to a boil.
Stir in shrimp and crabmeat. Cook about 15 minutes - until shrimp is firm.
Fish out (ha, ha) the bay leaf.
Serve with hot rice.
Serves 10.

Barbecued Corn Chili

(*A nice change from the normal chili.*)

1 pound ground beef
1/2 cup chopped onion
1 tablespoon chili powder
1 teaspoon salt
1 clove crushed garlic
1 28-ounce can tomatoes, undrained
1 1-pound can kidney beans, undrained
1 12-ounce can corn, undrained
1 cup barbecue sauce (your choice)

Brown meat in soup pot. Stir in onion, chili powder, salt and garlic, sauteing until onion is tender. Stir in remaining ingredients. Cover. Simmer 20 minutes. Serves 8.

Cheddar Bread

(*If you want, brush some melted butter over the top of the bread when it comes out of the oven. Sprinkle with garlic salt.*)

3 1/3 cups Bisquick
2 cups shredded sharp cheddar cheese
1 1/4 cups milk
2 eggs

Combine Bisquick and cheese. Add milk and eggs, mixing just until moistened. Spread into greased 9x5-inch loaf pan. Bake at 350 degrees for 55 minutes.

Curried Tomato Soup

1 1-pound can whole tomatoes, undrained
1 small onion
1 small celery rib
1 teaspoon salt
1/4 teaspoon pepper
1 tablespoon butter
2 tablespoons cornstarch
1 tablespoon curry powder
1 1/2 cups milk
1 tablespoon tomato paste
1/2 cup cream
1 tablespoon sugar

Puree tomatoes, onion, celery, salt and pepper in food
processor or blender. Strain into a 2-quart saucepan.
Over low heat, cook mixture until simmering. In a 3-
quart saucepan over medium-low heat, melt butter; stir in
cornstarch and curry powder until smooth. Gradually stir
in milk until smooth. Stir constantly until mixture is
thickened. Slowly whisk in the hot tomato mixture, then
tomato paste, cream and sugar. Heat until serving
temperature - do not boil.
Serves 4.

Raisin Cinnamon Beer Bread

(If your crazy uncle is coming over, open two cans of beer and drink first.)

2 cups self-rising flour
1 cup whole wheat flour
1 1/2 teaspoons baking powder
1 teaspoon cinnamon
1/2 teaspoon nutmeg
1/8 teaspoon cloves
1 12-ounce can beer
1 tablespoon honey
1 cup raisins

Mix dry ingredients in large bowl until well blended. Add remaining ingredients, mixing well. Spread into greased 9x5-inch loaf pan. Bake at 350 degrees for 45 minutes or until nice and brown.

Irish Soda Bread

3 1/4 cups flour
1/4 cup sugar
1 teaspoon baking powder
1 teaspoon baking soda
1 teaspoon salt
1/2 cup butter
1 1/3 cups buttermilk
1/4 cups raisins
Sugar

Combine dry ingredients; cut in butter until mixture is crumbly. Mix in buttermilk and raisins, mixing just until moistened. Shape into ball. On floured surface, knead dough ten times. Shape into round loaf. Roll in sugar. Place on greased cookie sheet. Cut deep cross into top. Bake at 350 degrees for 1 hour.

Creamy Shrimp and Rice Casserole

*(A little bit of work here, but the results are fantastic.
A unique blend of flavors.)*

1/4 cup green pepper
1/4 cup chopped onion
2 tablespoons olive oil
2 tablespoons butter
1 tablespoon lemon juice
1 10 3/4- ounce can tomato soup
1 cup whipping cream
2 cups cooked rice
1/8 teaspoon mace
1/8 teaspoon pepper
1/8 teaspoon paprika
1 1/2 pounds medium peeled and cooked shrimp
1/2 cup sliced almonds, divided

In a large skillet, saute green pepper and onion in butter
and oil for 5 minutes.   Stir in lemon juice, soup, cream,
rice, mace, pepper and paprika.   Stir in shrimp and 1/4
cup almonds.   Pour into a 2- quart baking dish.
Bake uncovered at 350 degrees
for 30 minutes.   Sprinkle
remaining almonds on top.
Bake for 20 minutes longer
or until casserole is
lightly browned.
Serves 6.

*This is stuff my brother and I make when I visit him in Virginia,
which I consider banjo country. Most of these recipes work well
at Thanksgiving, which is usually when I make my trek to
Richmond. You will not find a recipe for grits - plain, cheese,
garlic or any other way. My lack of appreciation for them is a
Yankee flaw that I've learned to live with.*

Curried Pecans

(Good to have around for munching, although they won't be
around for long)

1 tablespoon salad oil
1- 1/2 teaspoon curry powder
1- 1/2 teaspoon Worcestershire sauce
1 pound shelled pecans

Heat the oil in a medium- sized skillet. Add curry powder
and Worcestershire sauce, blending well. Add pecans;
stir until coated. Cook over medium heat for 5 minutes.
Spread in a single layer on a cookie sheet and bake at 300
degrees for 20 minutes.

Green Bean Salad

(A make-ahead, different kind of salad. Something you can pick at whenever you open the fridge.)

2 pounds cooked green beans
1/4 teaspoon sugar
3/4 cup vinegar
1/4 cup salad oil
1 tablespoon garlic salt
1/4 teaspoon pepper
1-1/2 teaspoons oregano

Place green beans in a bowl. Shake remaining ingredients in a jar and pour over beans. Mix well. Chill overnight. Serve on lettuce leaves or alone as a side dish. Serves 6-8.

Oyster Stuffing

(Our turkey is always stuffed with this.)

1 cup butter
2 cups finely chopped onion
2 cups thinly sliced celery
3 loaves bread
4 teaspoons chopped parsley
2 teaspoons salt
1 teaspoon pepper
4 teaspoons sage - or to taste
1 quart oysters, drained

Melt butter in a skillet. Add onion and celery; cook until soft - about 5 minutes. Cut crusts from bread and tear bread into crumbs in a large bowl. Pour onion-celery mixture over bread and mix thoroughly - you'll have to use you hands to really get in there. Add parsley, salt, pepper, and sage. Mix in oysters. You'll have enough for a 20-25 pound turkey.

Peanut Soup

(We eat this at Thanksgiving dinners. Actually, we make it an hour or two before dinner is ready and wolf it down while waiting for everything else to finish baking and cooking. It's very rich - a small amount goes a long way. Here's enough for everyone at your table.)

1/4 cup butter
1 minced onion
1 cup diced celery
3 tablespoons flour
8 cups chicken broth
2 cups peanut butter (chunky or smooth - your choice)
1 cup light cream
Salt and pepper
Chopped parsley
Chopped peanuts

Sauté onion and celery in butter until soft. Stir in flour until well blended. Add chicken broth, stirring constantly, and bring to a boil. Turn heat to low and stir in peanut butter. Remove from stove and add the cream. See if it needs salt or pepper. (Sometimes the peanut butter is salty enough on its own.) When ready to serve, top with parsley and chopped peanuts. Serves 10.

Oyster Stew

(We eat this the day after Thanksgiving to use all those extra oysters we bought for the stuffing.)

1-1/2 pints oysters and oyster liquid
5 tablespoons butter
3 cups milk (or a mixture of milk and cream)
Salt and pepper to taste
Cayenne pepper

Cook oysters and butter in a large saucepan until the edges of the oysters curl. Stir in milk and heat; do not boil. Season with salt and pepper. Ladle into soup dishes and garnish with cayenne pepper. Serves 4-6.

Corn Bread

(Serve with or without butter - either way, it will disappear.)

1 cup corn meal
1/4 cup flour
1 tablespoon sugar
1 teaspoon salt
1 teaspoon baking powder
1/2 teaspoon baking soda
1 cup buttermilk
1 beaten egg
2 tablespoons bacon grease or salad oil

Mix dry ingredients in a large bowl. Pour in buttermilk, egg and grease; beat well. Pour into a well-greased 8-inch square pan. Bake at 425 degrees for 25-30 minutes. Cut into squares.

Virginia Crab Cakes

(I like this recipe because it is not as bready — translate to sawdust — tasting as some cakes)

1 pound crab meat
1 tablespoon mayonnaise
1 beaten egg
Salt and pepper to taste
Worcestershire to taste
Bread crumbs
4-6 tablespoons butter

Mix crab meat, mayonnaise, egg, salt, pepper and Worcestershire sauce. Form into small cakes. Dip both sides of the cakes into the bread crumbs. Melt butter in a skillet and fry cakes over medium heat until light brown. Serves 4.

Red Velvet Cake

(Yee-haw. A real banjo-pickin' favorite.)

1/2 cup shortening	2 1/2 cups sifted cake flour
1 1/2 cups sugar	1 cup buttermilk
2 eggs	1 teaspoon salt
1 teaspoon vanilla	1 tablespoon vinegar
3 tablespoons cocoa	1 teaspoon baking soda
2 ounces of red food coloring	

Cream shortening, sugar, eggs and vanilla. Make a paste of cocoa and food coloring. Add to first mixture. Alternately add flour and buttermilk. Mix baking soda and vinegar in small bowl. Add to the batter, blending well. Bake in three 8-inch pans for 20-25 minutes at 350 degrees. Let cool completely. Fill and cover with frosting.

Frosting:

(You can double if you like a thicker coating on your cake.)

6 ounces softened
  cream cheese
6 tablespoons butter
1 teaspoon vanilla
2 cups sifted powdered sugar

Beat all ingredients until smooth. If desired, stir in 1/2 cup chopped pecans.

Chocolate Bourbon Pecan Pie

(Stand back!!!)

1 cup sugar
1/4 cup melted butter
3 slightly beaten eggs
3/4 cup light corn syrup
1/4 teaspoon salt
2 tablespoons bourbon
1 teaspoon vanilla
1/2 cup chopped pecans
1/2 cup chocolate chips
1 8-inch pie shell

Cream sugar and butter. Add eggs, syrup, salt, bourbon and vanilla. Mix until blended. Spread pecans and chocolate chips in bottom of pie shell.
Pour filling into shell.
Bake for 40-50 minutes
 at 375 degrees.

-- APRIL --

Time is
on my side

April.   Time to spring ahead.   Tempus fugit,
particularly this month.   Or, you could be like me and
never know what time it is.

I was given a Cinderella watch in a tiny glass slipper for
my fifth birthday.   It was so cool that I became forever
hooked on watches and clocks.   I now own ten clocks,
eight wristwatches, and one pocket watch.   Not one tells
the correct time.

I will wear a wristwatch until the batteries run down,
the stem winder breaks or the band gives out.   Then I
throw it into my purse where I carry it with the others,
always sure I will pass a jewelry store or watch shop (are
there such things anymore?) where I can procure whatever
is needed to get it operational again.   In the meantime, I
buy another watch for 10 bucks to get by.   The first thing I
do is set it ahead five to 10 minutes, since I'm always late
to everything.   When daylight savings time rolls around in
the fall, I leave it where it is, banking the hour until I
really need it.   For about two weeks I am 50 minutes early
to everything.   Then I catch on and mentally add 70
minutes to my schedule, while never changing my watch.

In April, my watch is sort of where it should be.
Last month I was in Meijer's when my watchband broke.
"Aha," I cleverly thought, "I will go to the jewelry counter
and buy a new watchband." As the store clerk pulled a
band out of the case, she told me it was $12. 95.
Shocked, I asked her the price of watches on a rack.
"Those are $9. 95," was the answer. So the old timer was
retired to my portable watch cemetery and I saved three
dollars by buying the watch - and I got a new watchband in
the deal.

She peered at the watches in my purse. "How many
have you got in there?" "Eight, now," I answered. "Do
you collect them?" "Not on purpose." She asked if I
wanted her to put batteries in the ones that needed them.
I thought about it a minute. "If I did that, all the
batteries would stop at once and I would be right back
where I started about a year from now. So... I'll just save
myself the trouble of having to do it all over again next
year and not get them fixed," I said, snapping my purse
shut. It made sense to me.

My clocks are in similar states. My grandfather clock
gongs six times when it's seven after four. A cheesy tiny
clock radio in the kitchen obtained free from MasterCard
buzzes at 6:45 a. m. daily. A British brass thing I got at a
flea market on Portabello Road dings whenever it wants.
An acquaintance, known for her freeloading ability, came
to spend "some time" recently, sleeping on my couch. She
left after one sleepless night. "All that buzzing and
gonging drove me nuts," she complained, throwing her
things into a suitcase. Clocks do serve their purpose.

As for getting up in the morning at a reasonable time, I
do not depend on anything as unreliable as a clock.
Instead my 13- pound cat, Hermes, sits on my head when
it is time to get up. He remains firmly implanted on my
face, closing off all breathing passages, until I get up to
feed him. It works much better than any alarm clock I
know.

Well, on to the kitchen, where my cat clock with the
moving rhinestone tail and eyes keeps me company. It
says the time is 2:16. But who knows?

While there, I'll share some recipes with you. Some
contain - what else? - thyme. The rest are of the herbal
variety.

Chicken in Wine

(Everyone loves this. The best part is they think I spend hours in the kitchen concocting it. Ha! It takes about five minutes.)

1 chicken, cut up
1 can cream of mushroom soup
1/2 package dry onion soup mix
1/4 teaspoon dried thyme
1/2 cup dry white wine

Place chicken pieces in a baking dish. Mix other ingredients together and pour over chicken. Bake, uncovered, at 350 degrees for 1 hour. (This makes a nice gravy to serve over rice.)

Fried Pike With Tomatoes

(Something a little different to do with fish.)

4 pike fillets
1/3 cup flour
2 teaspoons tarragon
1 teaspoon salt
1/4 teaspoon pepper
1/3 cup butter
3 tomatoes, cut in wedges
1 teaspoon capers

Dip fillets into a mixture of flour, tarragon, salt and pepper. Heat butter in a large skillet and fry fillets until golden. Turn and move to the side of the skillet. Put tomatoes in skillet and sprinkle fish with capers. Cook until tomatoes are hot and fish is flaky.

Chicken Marinade

(You can use this on oven-baked chicken or, with grill-out time approaching, outside over the coals.)

3/4 cup salad oil
1/2 cup dry white wine
1 clove garlic, minced
1 onion, finely chopped
1/2 teaspoon garlic salt
1/2 teaspoon salt
1/2 teaspoon pepper
1/4 teaspoon thyme

Shake all ingredients in a covered jar; pour over the chicken pieces. Chill 3-4 hours, turning occasionally. Baste during baking with marinade.

Herb Butter

(Use this on popcorn,
Italian bread or corn on the cob -
or as a lubricant for a pokey time piece.)

1/2 cup butter
1 teaspoon dried basil
1 teaspoon dried chervil
1/2 teaspoon dried thyme

For popcorn: melt butter;
stir in herbs.

For bread or corn on the cob:
soften butter; beat in herbs.

Tarragon Vinegar

(A great change from the usual vinegar taste. Pour into decorative bottles for a nice hostess gift.)

3 tablespoons fresh tarragon
4 cups cider vinegar
4 whole cloves
2 garlic cloves

Gently warm all ingredients. Pour into a covered container; chill. After 24 hours, remove the garlic. Chill again. After 2 weeks, strain vinegar into sterile bottles and cork.

Cottage Cheese Dill Bread

*(I bet you can eat
this whole thing by yourself.
I did. I puffed up for
three days like the Pillsbury
Dough Boy, but hey -
that's what baggy sweat
suits are for.)*

1 package dry yeast
1/4 cup warm water
1 cup cottage cheese
1/4 cup shortening
2 tablespoons sugar
1 tablespoons minced onion
2 tablespoons dill seed
2 teaspoons salt
1/4 teaspoon baking soda
1 egg
2-1/2 cups flour

Soften yeast in water. Warm cottage cheese in saucepan.
Stir in shortening, sugar, onion, dill seed, salt, baking
soda and yeast. Beat in egg. Add flour, a little at a time,
to make a soft dough. Knead on floured board until
smooth, about 10 minutes. Put in greased bowl, turning
once to grease top. Cover with a towel and let rise in
warm place 1 hour. Punch down. Cover and let rest 10
minutes. Place in greased loaf pan. Cover and let rise
again until about double, about 30-45 minutes. Bake at
350 degrees for about 50 minutes.

That inscrutable smile - those crepe suzettes!

(And, since the French also flew a flag over Michigan, it seems appropriate that I relate a story of traveling in France.)

Look for me at the East Lansing Art Festival because...I'm an art lover. I possess an Elvis toothpick holder, a photo of Richard Nixon playing a Spinet, and a 1930s platform shoe to prove it. Great art? It could be...somewhere.

My most cherished possession, however, is a plastic, gold-toned framed octagonal Mona Lisa tacked up inside my hall closet. I looked for years at the Art Festival for something of this quality without success. So, awhile back daughter Jessica and I headed for, where else?, France to find the perfect object d'art.

We rented a Volvo during rush hour in Paris, hoping to spot a suitable work of art along the Seine. After two hours of navigating one-way streets the wrong way, mowing down shrubbery on sidewalks and narrowly avoiding oncoming buses, we headed out of town.

We located the sun in the west and drove south to a city called Blois, pronounced "Blah" as best we could determine. We spent the evening on the city hall steps watching the horn section of a local band. The trumpeters all puffed on cigarettes during the concert, balancing their smokes on music stands. They took long drags on their cigarettes in between blows on their trumpets. We fully expected smoke to pour forth from those golden bells. Fascinating. That evening we ate frites and chicken in a local café. My wine came in a cruet, which I mistook for vinegar. I dumped the contents on my fries. Eeii, Americans.

The next day we found a souvenir shop called "Michigan" – run by people who had no idea what Michigan was – which sold Blois trinkets. But we could not find the great work of art we were searching for.

On the road, we stopped at a frite stand for some fries and a Coke. The proprietor quickly determined we were Americans who spoke no French. He spoke no English. But we could all speak a bit of Spanish. Our conversation went something like this: "You girls should not be on this road. It very dangerous to be alone. " "Why? Where we? " "Nowhere. " "Oh. Where somewhere? "

He asked if we had a map. Jessica brought forth a crumpled paper from beneath the seat. I asked him for "very small fries and a Coke. " He heaped a pile into a paper cone, smiled at us, and then heaped on some more. A kilo of frites.

When he wasn't looking, I would drop two or three under his stand, grinding them into the ground. I didn't want to hurt his feelings. Then, in a touching gesture, he rummaged around in a box and pulled out a Louis Armstrong tape. "You like him? " he asked. "Yes. He is good. " "He's the best. " "Yes, he's the bestest. "

The man smoothed out the map and pointed to a town. "You go there. " "It be nice? " "Yes. Very nice.

And only 30 kilometers. " "Okay. Thank you. Good-
bye. " "Hey, you forgot your frites. "

We went to the town. It be nice. But it didn't have
our artwork.

A few days later we arrived in Nice, tired and hungry.
We set out for dinner when we saw *it* in the corner window
of a closed sourvenir shop. The gold-toned octagonal
Mona Lisa. She looked at us with eyes that said: "Get me
outta here. " The next morning we beat it into the shop at
10 a. m. When I pointed to the picture, the clerk said
something like: "Okay. Finally. Some *really* stupid
tourists. " We raced back to the hotel with our purchase.
With our TV blaring "Roulette de la Fortune, " and
Nanette turning the letters in the background, we hung
our treasure over the television – it seemed so appropriate.
We carried that picture throughout France and beyond,
hanging it on our hotel walls. We often wondered what
the chambermaids thought. We worried at various
customs borders that they would mistake it for the real
thing.

And getting back to the States
is a whole other story. It would
not fit in the overhead bin or
under the seat...or anywhere
else. It spent an unscheduled
night in New York City and
bounced between four airports
before finally arriving in East
Lansing. But it was all
worth it. Now I have a
work of art in my closet that
shouts to all who open that
door: "Get me outta here. "

Recipes are,
what else, French.

Crepe Suzettes

(The best crepes in the world are served at a crepe stand near the Odeon metro stop in Paris. The man piles on the filling, so you can walk down the street with goo running down the front of your shirt. He'll rustle up anything from ham and cheese to strawberry crepes, but my favorite is this old stand-by.)

Crepes

4 eggs	1/2 cup milk
1/2 cup water	2 tablespoons butter
1 cup flour	3/4 teaspoon salt
1 tablespoon sugar	1 teaspoon vanilla

Beat eggs with a whisk. Beat in remaining ingredients, one at a time. Let batter stand one hour. Heat a skillet until hot. Brush bottom of skillet with butter; pour about 2 tablespoons batter into the pan. Turn and tip the pan immediately so that the batter forms a thin film over the bottom. After 15-20 seconds, lift to see if the bottom has browned. If so, flip it over. Cook for another 10-15 seconds. Slide onto a warmed plate. Continue on…you'll get the hang of it. Makes 2-3 dozen, depending on size.

Flavored Butter

For 12 crepes, cream together 1/4 cup butter and 1/4 cup powdered sugar. Take one orange and grate the outer peel; add to the creamed mixture. Stir in the juice from the orange. Mix in 3 tablespoons Grand Marnier.

The Finished Product

Heat the flavored butter in a large skillet. Using a fork and spoon, dip each crepe into the butter mixture; fold into quarters and move to one side of the pan. Repeat with remaining crepes. Sprinkle crepes with 3 more tablespoons Grand Marnier and a little sugar. (In restaurants, servers add a little more booze and set the whole thing on fire at this point. However, seeing as how I would set myself on fire if I tried this, I simply remove the crepes to dessert plates and serve, forgetting the dramatics.)

Roasted Chicken
with Tarragon

(Your whole house will smell divine — neighbors will be hanging outside your windows wearing "please-invite-me-in" expressions.)

(1) 5-6-pound roasting chicken
Lemon
Salt
6 tablespoons butter
2 sprigs fresh tarragon (or 1/2 teaspoon dried)

Wash chicken. Rub inside and out with a cut lemon and salt. Put 5 tablespoons butter and a sprig (1/4 teaspoon dried) of tarragon inside the cavity. Crush sprig of tarragon between fingers; mix tarragon flavor (or 1/4 teaspoon dried) with 1 tablespoon butter. Rub skin of chicken with butter-tarragon mixture. Roast chicken on its side at 375 degrees for 30 minutes. Turn to the other side and baste with drippings. Roast for another 30 minutes. Baste again and roast for 30 more minutes, or until chicken is done.

French Dressing

(So basic, so good.)

One part wine vinegar to 3 parts olive oil; 1/2 teaspoon salt, 1/8 teaspoon pepper, 1/2 teaspoon mustard. Put in a jar and shake. That's it! Add your own touches. For instance, add garlic and/or Worcestershire sauce for zip. Add basil for tomatoes, chervil for potato salad, dill for cucumbers, a blend of herbs and Roquefort cheese for mixed greens. Have fun with it.

Chocolate Mousse

(There was once a touristy restaurant on the Champs-Elysees. The reason for frequenting this establishment was for their chocolate mousse which was served properly ... at least to me ... in a punch bowl with a large serving spoon. The bowl was placed on your table so you could eat three, four, five portions. Burp. No wonder it went out of business.)

4 squares (ounces) unsweetened chocolate
3/4 cup sugar
1/3 cup milk
6 eggs, separated
1-1/2 cups butter
1-1/2 cups powdered sugar
1/8 teaspoon salt
1-1/2 teaspoons vanilla extract

Melt chocolate in top part of a double boiler over hot water. Mix sugar, milk and egg yolks; add to the chocolate, stirring constantly over the heat until smooth and thickened. Cool. Cream butter and 3/4 cup powdered sugar. Add to the cooled chocolate mixture, beating well. Beat egg whites with salt until stiff; gradually beat in remaining 3/4 cup powdered sugar. Fold into chocolate mixture. Stir in vanilla. Chill overnight. Garnish with whipped cream and shaved chocolate, if desired. Serves a lot.

Orange Duck

(1) 5-pound duckling
Salt and pepper
1 tablespoon grated orange peel
1/2 cup chicken stock
1 teaspoon cornstarch
1/4 cup orange juice
1/4 cup white wine

Sprinkle inside of duck with salt and pepper.   Truss bird
and put on rack in roasting pan.   Add orange peel to
chicken stock.   Pour over duck; roast uncovered at 325
degrees for 3 hours, basting occasionally with liquid in
bottom of pan.   When duck is done, remove to hot
serving platter.   Pour off all but 1/2 cup of the liquid.
Stir cornstarch into orange juice
until blended.   Stir into
sauce with wine and
cook on top of stove,
stirring until thickened.
Pour over duck.

PACIFIC·97®
World Philatelic Exhibition
San Francisco, California
29 May-8 June

1 Sept. 1999

have mock

I've
mo

PAPUA NEW

Carole Eberly
1334 Michigan Ave.
E. Lansing, MI 48823

USA
COUNTRY OF DESTINATION

AEROGRAMME

hen I get back.
get really homesick
I my age and all and I would
him - I need a friend who's not a
acceptable for men and women to be fr
live right next door to each other, I'm not a
and tell him that line of "The Gambler"
Anyway, only 3 more weeks and I
I love you!

— Jessi

P.S. Could you send me another black
really sun bleached.

First Fold Here

PAPUA NEW

25t

PAPUA N

The toughest job I'll ever love

*The Peace Corps has a way
of making you grow up.*

Daughter Jessica is in Papua New Guinea -- I had to look it up in the atlas, too -- with the Peace Corps. All I knew about the country was a Rockefeller disappeared there, it was the scene of some nasty South Pacific fighting during the war and it outlawed cannibalism earlier this century. Now I know it has about 4 million people, 800 languages and my daughter. But, through her letters, I'm learning more about the beautiful Highlands, where she is currently stationed before being sent elsewhere in PNG to teach high school science. I know she lives in a bamboo hut, eats lots or rice and sweet potatoes, bathes in a river, and attends a church that has a statue with a golden head and things that look like running shoes. Her Tok Pism is good, she says. She spends evenings sitting on a dirt floor sharing stories with her host family, who is very kind. The villagers have renamed her Helenou, meaning "legend." She has not heard "Jessica" since she has been there.

I'm also learning much more about myself. We are so far apart -- 14 hours of time difference and an equator separate us -- that there is no time or space in our letters for anything but complete honesty. Once we cover the daily happenings -- the grand opening of the Albert Street parking lot, her contribution to high-tech (a kerosene lantern she took with her) -- we get down to what's really important. Life, love, dreams, plans, philosophical wanderings of the mind. Jessica, so strong, courageous and adventurous, asks for my support. "Am I doing the right thing?" Me, so flip, capricious and spontaneous, doling out advice. "This is where you should be at this point in your life." Who appointed me wise guy (woman)? When did I get old enough to become Ann Landers? When she was growing up, Jessica and I were more like sisters than mother and daughter. It was pure joy. Jessica was my excuse to reread Uncle Wiggily books, see goofy G-rated movies and proudly attend her concerts, plays and ballets. I would look at her at night as she slept and could not believe I was so blessed.

Now she is asking me important questions. And I have to come up with straight answers. Nothing cute or clever. It has to come from the heart. It gives me the willies. But, it also has added another dimension to my life. Now, I have to carefully explore what I tell her because this is, in part, what she is basing her life on. She's no slouch. She will know if I'm evading issues, being less than honest or not giving 100 percent of what I have learned on Planet Earth all these years.

I read and reread her aerogrammes until they hang torn at their creases, hoping to wring one more piece of information from them. I examine the handwriting, the

greeting, the stamp for some deeper meaning. She writes
of happiness, sadness, wonderment and loneliness. Then
I sit and write, offering her support, love and more
advice.

The toughest job I'll ever love.

Since I have no specific idea what culinary delights are offered in PNG, I offer some that use that country's staples -- sweet potatoes and rice. Sweet potatoes, as you know, are very good for you -- lots of vitamin A and other important things.

Sweet Potato Pudding

(This can be served as a vegetable or dessert. It tastes a lot like Indian pudding. Serve with whipped cream or ice cream if you decide to use it as a dessert.)

1 can (1 pound, 13 ounce) sweet potatoes, drained and mashed
1/2 cup butter, melted
1 cup sugar
1/2 cup milk
1 egg, beaten
3/4 teaspoon cinnamon
1/4 teaspoon cloves
1/4 teaspoon nutmeg

Stir all ingredients together except nutmeg. Pour into buttered 2 1/2 quart casserole; sprinkle with nutmeg. Bake at 350 degrees for 45 minutes. Serves 6.

Grilled Sweet Potatoes

(A nice change from baked white potatoes.)

Take two large sweet potatoes and cut in half. Place each on a piece of tin foil large enough for wrapping. Sprinkle each cut side with 1 tablespoon brown sugar, a dash of cinnamon, nutmeg and ginger, 1 tablespoon butter and 2 teaspoons water. Wrap each potato tightly. Place in coals and bake for about 20 minutes, turning once. Poke with a knife to see if they're done. If not, put them back for more baking. If they are, unwrap and eat. They may be burned a little, but that's part of the grilling experience, right?

Sweet Potato Pie

Traditionally, a Thanksgiving pie. But, what the heck.

3 eggs
1 cup sugar
1 cup cooked sweet potato, beaten
3/4 cup evaporated milk
1/4 cup milk
1/4 cup butter, melted
1 teaspoon pumpkin pie spice
2 teaspoons vanilla
10 inch pie shell, unbaked

Beat together eggs, sugar and sweet potatoes. Add milks, butter, spice and vanilla. Pour into pastry shell and bake at 400 degrees for 10 minutes; then at 325 degrees for 30 minutes more. When knife inserted in center comes out clean, the pie is done.

Sweet Potato and Apple Bake

4 large sweet potatoes   6 apples
1 cup sugar   1/2 cup butter
1 cup hot water

Scrub potatoes and let boil until done. Peel; slice into thick slices. Pare and slice apples into thick pieces. Layer in casserole dish with half the potatoes at bottom, cover with half the apples, sprinkle with half the sugar and butter. Repeat. Pour in hot water. Bake at 350 degrees about 30 minutes, or until apples are done. Serves 6-8.

Arroz Brasileiro (Brazilian Rice)

(I lived in Brazil as a teenager and rice appeared on nearly everyone's dinning room table. This recipe, served with black beans, was a staple in the school lunch room. Good.)

2 tablespoons lard or vegetable fat
1 small onion, chopped
1/2 clove garlic, mined
3 tomatoes, peeled and chopped
1 bay leaf
2 cup uncooked, regular rice
1 teaspoon salt
3-4 cups boiling water

Stir together lard, onion, garlic, tomatoes and bay leaf. Add rice and salt. Stir until the rice absorbs the tomato mixture. Cover with boiling water. Cook over high heat for 5 minutes. Reduce heat, cover, and simmer. Cook until fluffy and tender. If the rice becomes too dry before it is tender, add a small amount of boiling water.

Chile Rice Casserole

(Different, tasty.)

6 cups cooked rice
1/2 pound Monterey Jack cheese, shredded
1 4-ounce can green chilies
2 teaspoons salt
1 teaspoon pepper
2 cups sour cream

In a large bowl, combine all ingredients except sour cream. Fold in sour cream. Spoon mixture into a greased 8-cup mold or bundt pan; pack lightly with back of spoon. Bake at 350 degrees for 30 minutes. Unmold on serving platter. Garnish with parsley, if desired.

Red Beans and Rice

(Good on a chilly day.)

1 1/2 pounds ground beef
3 cloves garlic, mined
1 cup onion, chopped
3 16-ounce cans kidney beans, undrained
2 16-ounce Italian-style tomatoes
1 16-ounce Cajun style tomatoes
1 4-ounce can sliced mushrooms
1 1/2 teaspoon salt
1 teaspoon pepper
1/2 teaspoon Tabasco sauce
2 tablespoons Worcestershire sauce
1/2 teaspoon onion powder
1/2 teaspoon garlic salt
1 12-ounce package Polish sausage (optional)
4 cups cooked white rice

In a large skillet, brown beef, garlic and onions; drain. Add beans, tomatoes, mushrooms and spices to ground beef. Simmer for 30 minutes. Cut sausage into bite-size pieces; brown in skillet until lightly crisp. Add to beans and simmer 10 minutes longer. Serve over hot rice. Serves 6-8.

Rice Pudding

(Umm, yummers.)

1/2 cup rice
1 cup water
1 quart whole milk
1/4 cup butter
3 eggs
1/2 cup sugar
1 cup raisins
1/2 teaspoon vanilla
1 tablespoon cinnamon

Cook rice in water for 7 minutes. Stir in milk and butter.
Simmer for 1 hour. Beat eggs; stir in sugar, raisins and
vanilla. Stir mixture slowly into rice mixture until pudding
thickens. Refrigerate. Serve cold with cinnamon
sprinkled over the top. Serves 4.

Spicy Shrimp and Rice

(Here's something Jessica might have had if she could have snagged some shrimp. It's a nice, hot-spicy dish. Actually she did catch her own fish for protein. She had no idea what variety they were - whatever swam up to her hook. She filleted them on the spot and cooked them over coals.)

3/4 pounds peeled shrimp
2 1/3 cups chicken broth
4 sliced green onions
1 teaspoon Worcestershire sauce
2 cloves minced garlic
1 teaspoon Tabasco sauce
2 cups stewed tomatoes
1 cup long grain rice
Salt
Pepper

Rinse shrimp and devein. Set aside. In a large frying pan, combine broth, green onions, Worcestershire sauce, garlic and Tabasco. Bring to a boil. Stir in tomatoes and rice. Return to a boil; reduce heat. Cover and simmer 15- 20 minutes or until rice is just tender, stirring once or twice. Stir in shrimp. Cover and simmer for 3- 5 minutes or until shrimp turns pink. Salt and pepper to taste. Makes 4 servings.

I'm in love with northern Michigan

One of the reasons I love Michigan so much is because summer is summer, winter is winter, spring is spring and autumn is autumn. No doubt about it. No wimpy 70-degree winters. No balmy, 65-degree summers – at least in Lansing. And everything in between prepares you for what is to follow. Only the hardiest survive.

My fondest memories of summer are in the pre-air conditioned, -condo, -mall days of the 1940s and 1950s. Summer consisted of walking uptown (Dearborn – Detroit was downtown) to drink cherry cokes for a nickel at the drug store, exploring the riverbank behind my house for Indian arrow heads and riding bikes with my brother to the Seashore Pool. No planned activities – except an occasional picnic at Belle Isle with a Leonard Smith concert and our annual family trips to Bob-Lo and the Detroit Zoo. Certainly no – God forbid – educational programs. No nothing. Just waking up each day to . . . well, nothing. If things reached the boredom level, mom always had a solution – clean your room. It was her own Head Start Program. If you got a head start, you could be out of the house before she brought the subject up again.

And there was always the annual odyssey Up North. No one has ever actually located Up North, but every Michigander knows where it is. It's Up North.

Preparations for our one-week vacation began a month prior to the trip. Mom cleaned the house from the curtains to the kitchen floor, making it acceptable to any burglar who wanted to break into a modest brick bungalow. Clothes were packed in suitcases. Bedding and towels found comfortable homes in boxes. Food, just is case there was none Up North, rattled around in brown paper A&P bags. Then, of course, there were the Monopoly and Rook games, fishing rods and AAA maps.

It's a good thing my dad was an engineer because it took all his skills to cram this junk into our maroon Studebaker. Besides that, he had to figure out how my brother and I would to sit elbow-to-elbow in the back seat without killing each other before we reached our destination.

Ah, but once the long trip was over . . . . The musty smell of the cabin near Elk Lake – the perfume of vacation time. The ice box hung together on the front porch, the sagging beds sagged a little more than the year before, four mismatched chairs completed the dining set. Heaven.

"Race ya to the beach," were the first words out of my brother's mouth. Carefully packed clothes went flying around the room in search of bathing suits.

Days were spent at the beach, reading books on the front porch or just hanging around town. The drug store was a favorite haunt because it contained comic books and three-inch-high wax bottles filled with red, green and purple syrup. While reading "Archie" and "Superman" comic books at the rack, Billy and I bit off the wax bottle tops to drink the syrupy liquid – finest vintage. Then we popped the bottles into our mouths and chewed them like gum. Actually, they tasted more like the paraffin mom put on jelly jars, but what the heck. We were Up North and things were just plain better.

One day we picked some red cherries along the road coming in from town. Mom made the best cherry pie I tasted – before or since – with an oven that had seen more of a workout than an Interstate Wendy's grill.

Billy and my dad went fishing every so often. Once, they even caught a fish. I found it flopping around the kitchen floor as it escaped the pail, searching for a way back to the stream. Dad heard my screams and promptly collared the poor fellow, filleting him on the spot. Must admit, he tasted pretty good.

Evenings found us around the kitchen table playing Monopoly, each trying to land on Boardwalk first. You just KNEW whoever bought Boardwalk would win the game. You could be up to your ears in mortgages, pick up the "Go Directly to Jail, Do Not Pass Go" card, and be out of money. Not to worry. Sooner or later Boardwalk would come through.

We even got to drink Rock 'n' Rye on those evenings. At home it was always Vernor's down at the Detroit plant, watching the bottling take place. But Up North was Rock 'n' Rye territory. Bags of pretzels and New Era potato chips topped off this gluttonous travel into gourmet-land.

Ah, summer.
No wonder teachers went
crazy around May.

Recipes are, of course,
summertime fare.

Lemonade Syrup

(You can make lemonade just like at the county fair with this recipe. It's easy to make a glass or a pitcher. Keep in the fridge for thirst emergencies.)

1 cups water
3 cups sugar
3 cups lemon juice
3 tablespoons lemon peel

Heat water to boiling. Stir in sugar until it dissolves. Cool. Stir in lemon juice and peel. Store in refrigerator for up to 1 week. To make 1 serving, mix 1/3 cup syrup with 3/4 cup cold water in a glass. Stir will. To make 8 servings, mix 2 2/3 cups syrup and 5 cups cold water in a 2-quart pitcher. Stir well.

Chilled Cucumber Buttermilk Soup

(Refreshing.)

7 cups buttermilk
3 tablespoons chopped chives
1 peeled cucumber, seeded and finely chopped
1 teaspoon dill
3 tablespoons chopped parsley
Salt and pepper to taste

Stir buttermilk and chives together and let stand for 30 minutes. Mix cucumber, dill and parsley together and let stand for 30 minutes. Combine all ingredients with salt and pepper. Chill thoroughly. Makes 6-8 servings.

Smoked Salmon
Dill Spread

(Spread this on crackers for appetizers or on bread for sandwiches. It's a snap to make.)

8 ounces cream cheese
1 7 1/2- ounce can salmon, drained and deboned
1/4 cup mayonnaise
1 tablespoon lemon juice
1 tablespoon grated onion
2 teaspoons horseradish
1/2 teaspoon dill weed
1/4 teaspoon salt
1/4 teaspoon liquid smoke
Fresh parsley for garnish if used for appetizers

Beat cream cheese until smooth. Stir in remaining ingredients, except parsley. Spread on crackers and garnish with parsley to make a pretty platter. Spread on bread of your choice – make it interesting – for sandwiches. Makes about 2 1/4 cups.

Italian Bread
& Chicken Salad

(Easy and a good way to use up the rest of a roasted chicken. On those hot summer days, this will get you in and out of the kitchen in a snap.)

1/3 cup olive oil
1/4 cup red wine vinegar
1/2 teaspoon garlic powder
1/2 teaspoon salt
4 teaspoon pepper
1 tablespoon Italian seasoning
5 cups day-old bread, cut into 1-inch pieces
4 tomatoes, cut into wedges
4 sliced green onions
1 pound cooked chicken
6 cups greens (Romaine lettuce works well)

In a large bowl combine oil, vinegar, garlic, salt, pepper and seasoning. Add bread, tomatoes and green onions. Toss well. Tear chicken into 1/2-inch thick strips. Cut greens into bite-size pieces. Add chicken and greens to bread mixture. Toss well. Let stand 20 minutes before serving. Makes 4 servings.

Beer-Battered Fish

1 cup Bisquick
1 cup beer
Salt and pepper to taste
2-3 pounds of fillets
Oil for frying

Mix Bisquick, beer, salt and pepper in a pan.
Dip fillets in mixture and fry in hot oil until golden brown. Drain on paper towels. Makes 4-6 servings.

Vegetable-Cottage Cheese Salad

(Spruce up that cottage cheese.)

1 cup water
1/2 cup olive oil
1/2 cup lemon juice
1 teaspoon onion salt
1 teaspoon oregano
1/2 teaspoon dried basil
1 clove minced garlic
Dash of pepper
2 cups carrot sticks
2 cups zucchini sticks
2 cups cauliflowerettes
Cottage cheese

Heat to a boil the water, olive oil, lemon juice, onion salt, oregano, basil, garlic and pepper. Stir in vegetables and boil about 4 minutes. Chill vegetables in marinade at least three hours. Drain and serve vegetables over individual servings of cottage cheese. Makes 4 servings.

Black and Blue Sauce

(Serve hot or cold over pancakes, waffles, ice cream, cake or pudding.)

3 cups blackberries
3 cups blueberries
1 cup water
2 cups sugar
1/2 cup corn syrup
1/4 teaspoon salt
Dash cinnamon
1 tablespoon cornstarch
2 tablespoon cold water
1 tablespoon lemon juice

Bring blackberries, blueberries and water to a boil. Simmer until berries are slightly softened, about 5-7 minutes. Add sugar, corn syrup, salt and cinnamon. Boil again. Mix cornstarch with cold water and stir into berries. Simmer until mixture is slightly thickened, about 5 minutes. Cool and stir in lemon juice. Makes about 5 cups.

Strawberry Pudding

(Try this instead of strawberry shortcake sometime.)

3 cups hulled strawberries
1 cup sugar
1/2 cup water
6 slices firm white bread
Butter
Whipped cream

Cook strawberries, sugar and water. Butter bread on one side. Cut into quarters. Alternate layers of bread and strawberry mixture in a loaf pan. Chill. Slice and serve with whipped cream.

Zucchini-Cheese Casserole

(*A way to use up all that zucchini.*)

3 sliced medium zucchini
2 tablespoons oil
1 teaspoon dried basil
1/3 cup grated
Parmesan cheese

1/2 cup chopped onion
1 pound cottage cheese
1/2 teaspoon oregano
1/4 teaspoon salt
2 peeled and sliced
tomatoes

Sauté zucchini and chopped onion in oil. Beat cottage cheese with basil, oregano and salt. Place alternating layers of zucchini, cottage cheese and tomatoes in a 2-quart casserole dish. Top with Parmesan cheese. Bake at 350 degrees uncovered for 25-30 minutes. Makes 6 servings.

Cherry Bran Muffins

(*Always room for anything with Michigan cherries in it.*)

1 egg
1/4 cup oil
2 cups bran cereal
1/8 teaspoon salt
2 teaspoons baking powder

1/2 cup milk
1 cup pitted sour cherries
1/2 cup sugar
1 cup sifted flour
1/2 teaspoon nutmeg

Combine egg, milk and oil. Stir in cherries and cereal. In a separate bowl, stir the sugar, salt, flour, baking powder and nutmeg. Add to the egg mixture, stirring just until moistened. Fill greased muffin tins 2/3 full and bake at 400 degrees for about 20 minutes. Makes about 12.

The price
is right

*(Although neither the Turks nor Chinese few a flag
over Michigan, I included this because…
well, I like a bargain.)*

Bargaining is one of the simple pleasures of life. I've
bargained for rugs in Izmir, aquamarines in Sao Paulo and
silver bracelets in Mexico. Anyone, I figure, can pay
retail. But, it's the belief that each party got the best deal
that makes parting with money fun. Americans, I
believe, would rather pay the sticker price than bargain —
just look at the complaints about car dealers. Many of my
friends are appalled when shopping with me. I will try
anything (senior citizen discounts, old coupons, the
"dented model" ruse) to get the price down on a desired
object.

But, back to the street. The antics involved in face-
to-face negotiations are street theater at its finest. One
summer day I wandered through the Grand Bazaar in
Istanbul. I found nothing of interest until I walked outside
and down the street a bit. There I spotted six small crystal
and gold glasses that would look great with my collection of
junk back home. I asked the price — outrageous. We
went back and forth, but I still was not sold. I walked
away. He came running after me. "Strong glasses," the

merchant said. I looked at him quizzically. "Look. Strong," he tugged at my arm. The seller placed the glasses in two rows upside down and then stood on them. "Strong," he said, arms waving in the air as he balanced himself. "Good and strong." Well, I could obviously see the advantage of having glasses I could stand on at home — might need them to reach a burned out light bulb.

Another fun place to bargain is China, where private enterprise is taking hold like a vengeance. Unless you find yourself in a state owned enterprise store, marked prices are suggested retail only — it's every shop and stall owner for him or herself. One bright, sunny day I wandered through the Silk Market near the embassies. After snagging three red Mao lighters that played annoying tunes upon opening (total cost less than $10), I saw my real love — a Women's Red Brigade alarm clock. You wound it up and a woman waved her arm in what I supposed was a Red Power salute. Tres cool. I picked it up, the universal signal that a sucker is about.

The stall keeper was on me. "Good clock," she said. She pointed out such features as the large hand and small hand, the two bells on top that rang (she demonstrated this), the knob for setting the time and the handy legs it rested on. She whipped out a calculator and punched in $10.

Now, this is where finesse takes over on the part of the buyer. "Hmm," I stared at the figure. Timing is everything. Too short of a stare and you could annoy the seller, risking having to pay full retail. Too long and you both could fall asleep. I held out my hand for the calculator. I punched in $4. "Ohhhhhh. Ohhhhhhh. Quality. Quality. Cannot do," she said. She again went through the features of the clock, turning the bells on and off. I stared at her with "Well, I am sort of interested" look. She punched in $8. Now, we were getting somewhere. But, this is the important part. I put the clock down and eyed her other wares with semi-interest.

She pointed out the other doo-dads. I shook my head — I wasn't interested. Then I went back to the clock. I smiled and held my hand out for the calculator. I punched in $5. "Ohhhhhhh. Ohhhhhhh. Quality clock. Cannot do. Quality." She feigned a heart attack. She took back the calculator and sighed. She smiled at me and fiddled with the comb in her hair. She punched in $7. "Best price," she said. I scratched my head, shuffled my feet, glanced at other stalls lining the street. "Hmmmmmm." I asked for the calculator. We stared at each other, motionless. I punched in $6. I handed it back to her and made the international gesture — a horizontal swipe through the air — that the haggling was over. She frowned at the figure, looked at me to make sure this was the end, then said, "Okay. But quality clock." We both laughed as the deal was struck. The fool and her money were parted. The whole transaction took close to ten minutes, but the entertainment value was worth the $6 — and I got a Women's Red Brigade clock thrown in. Now if only I could do that at Sear's.

Recipes are in honor of some the most savvy and fun bargainers I've come across — the Chinese. Warning: read these recipes thoroughly before starting; they seem confusing at first, but plunge ahead — they're really quite simple once you get the hang of it.

Braised Chicken Wings

*(A sweet — ha, ha — alternative to
the usual buffalo wings.)*

1 1/2 pounds chicken wings, cut into sections
1 cup Kikkoman soy sauce
1 cup water
1/2 cup brown sugar
1 cup sherry
4 scallions, cut in 3-inch sections

Bring soy sauce, water, sugar and sherry to a boil. Add
chicken wings and scallions. Simmer uncovered for 20-25
minutes. Serve as appetizers without the sauce or with
main meal with the sauce. Serve hot or cold.

String Beans and Garlic

3 cloves garlic
1 pound young string beans
2 tablespoons salad oil
4 tablespoons soy sauce
1 teaspoon sugar
1 tablespoon sherry

Peel and crush garlic. Wash, devein and snap beans into
2-inch sections. Heat oil in skillet; sauté garlic for 1
minute. Add in beans and stir for 2 minutes. Add soy
sauce, sugar, and sherry; stir for 2 more minutes. Cover
and cook for 5 minutes.

Mushrooms, Bamboo Shoots and Pea Pods

(Good enough to be a meal in itself.)

1/2 cup dried black mushrooms
1/2 pound pea pods
1/2 cup bamboo shoots
4 tablespoons salad oil
1/2 teaspoon salt
2 tablespoons soy sauce
1 teaspoon sugar
1/4 teaspoons MSG

Soak black mushrooms in enough boiling water to cover for 15 minutes. Squeeze out water, cut off and discard stems; slice the mushrooms into 1/4-inch strips. Devein pea pods and rinse. Slice bamboo shoots into 1/8-inch rectangular pieces. Heat 2 tablespoons of oil in skillet over high heat. Add salt and pea pods, stirring constantly until the pods turn dark green. Remove pods. In same skillet, heat remaining 2 tablespoons oil. Stir in bamboo shoots and mushrooms. Add soy sauce, sugar and MSG. Return the pea pods and stir.

Tomatoes, Onions and Beef

(Who can say they don't like Chinese food after eating this?)

1 pound flank steak	4 tablespoon soy sauce
1 tablespoon sugar	1 tablespoon sherry
1 1/2 tablespoons cornstarch	5 tomatoes
1 onion	1 tablespoon sugar
1 teaspoon salt	5 tablespoons salad oil
1 scallion,	1 tablespoon cornstarch
cut in 2-inch sections	1/2 cup water

Slice flank steak in 1 1/2x1-inch slices across the grain. Marinate in soy sauce, 1 tablespoon sugar, sherry and 1 1/2 tablespoons cornstarch for 15 minutes. Cut tomatoes into quarters. Cut onion into 1-inch chunks. In a skillet, heat 3 tablespoons salad oil. Sauté scallion 30 seconds, add meat and sauté until 2/3 brown and 1/3 pink. Remove into bowl. In same skillet, heat 2 tablespoons oil, sauté onions 1-2 minutes, breaking up the sections; add in tomatoes. Sauté for 2 minutes. Add 1 tablespoon sugar and salt. Mix 1 tablespoon cornstarch with 1/2 cup water; pour into skillet and stir until somewhat thickened. Add meat mixture.
Stir well.

Chicken or Pork Noodles
(AKA Chinese spaghetti.)

1/2 pound chicken or lean pork

Marinade mix:
4 1/2 tablespoons soy sauce
1/2 teaspoons sugar
1 teaspoon sherry
2 teaspoons cornstarch

1 carrot	1 green pepper
1 onion	2 stalks celery
3/4 cup bamboo shoots	5 black mushrooms
1 pound extra thin spaghetti	2 teaspoons salt
1 tablespoons sesame seed oil	6 tablespoons salad oil
1/2 cup water	1/4 teaspoons MSG
1 tablespoon cornstarch	1/2 tablespoons water

Shred chicken or pork and place in marinade mixture for
15- 20 minutes. Shred or chop fine carrot, green pepper,
onions, celery and bamboo shoots. Soak mushrooms in
boiling water for 15 minutes. Squeeze out water, cut off
and discard steams. Shred and set aside. Heat some
water to boiling with salt in a large pan and put in
spaghetti. Stir, bring to boil again; turn off heat. Cover
and let spaghetti sit 20- 25 minutes. Stir and drain. Mix
with sesame seed oil to prevent sticking. Heat 4
tablespoons salad oil in skillet, sauté carrots, onions and
green pepper for 2 minutes. Add celery, mushrooms,
bamboo shoots and MSG, sautéing for 1 minute. Remove
to separate bowl. Heat 2 tablespoons oil in same skillet.
Sauté marinated meat 1- 2 minutes; add 1/2 cup water.
Mix 1 tablespoon cornstarch with 1/2 tablespoon water.
Stir into mixture until thickened. Return vegetables to
skillet and mix well. Pour over cooked spaghetti and mix.

Egg Drop Soup

(Watching those calories? Try this.)

2 13-3/4 ounce cans chicken broth
2 cans water
1 1/2 teaspoons salt
1 slice ginger root
1 medium tomato quartered
1/2 teaspoon dry sherry
3 eggs
1 tablespoon diced scallions

Bring broth, water, salt, ginger root and tomato to a boil. Turn to low and simmer 5 minutes. In a small bowl, beat together sherry and eggs. Remove tomato peel and ginger root slice from soup stock. Bring soup to a boil; slowly stir in beaten egg mixture. Remove immediately from heat and garnish with diced scallions.

Fried Rice

(This is a recipe I wing; you can too.
Everything is more or less, which makes it great for leftovers.)

4-6 cups cooked rice
2 tablespoons salad oil
1 cup leftover cooked meat
1 small package peas and carrots
1-2 eggs, slightly beaten
Soy sauce to taste

Heat rice with oil in skillet until hot. Stir in cooked meat and peas and carrots. When hot, push mixture to sides of skillet, making a hole in the middle. You might have to put a little more oil in. Pour the eggs into the hole and cook, stirring once in awhile. When eggs are pretty much set, mix the whole thing around. Add soy sauce.

Chicken and Almonds

(Does food get any better?)

3 tablespoons salad oil
2 cups diced raw chicken
1 cup cooked peas
1/2 cup sliced mushrooms
1 teaspoon cornstarch
1/2 cup almonds

1 teaspoon salt
2 tablespoons soy sauce
1 cup diced celery
1 cup boiling water
1/2 cup cold water

Heat oil and salt in skillet. When very hot, add chicken and sauté for 3 minutes. Add soy sauce, peas, celery and mushrooms, stirring well. Very slowly add boiling water and stir. Cover skillet and cook about 4 minutes. Mix cornstarch with cold water and add to chicken mixture. Lower heat. When gravy thickens and becomes clear, remove from heat and pour onto serving dish. Sprinkle with almonds.

-- SEPTEMBER --

The thing from the garage sale

There's a round marble table top held aloft by two rococo plaster of Paris cherubs in my bathroom. It will be in my garage sale this month if you want it. I bought this piece in a moment of stupidity at another garage sale. I believe that useless items just float around neighborhoods via garage sales. They never find final resting places because someone, somewhere might just want them. "Hey, that's junk, but it's too good to throw out. Let's put it in a garage sale."

Daughter Jessica is busy furnishing her first apartment. Believing that garage sales were the way to go, she enlisted me in her bargain-hunting expeditions. I had been out of the loop for about a decade but, like all addictions, it was easy to get hooked again. With red pen in hand, I eagerly awaited Thursday's newspaper so I could circle all the sales we would hit Friday. After a few weeks we got so good at garage saling that we participated in drive- by "snootings. " This is for the experienced saler.   You peruse the stuff from your car.   If nothing looks enticing, you pretend you were actually looking for the address of someone important, put your nose up in the air and zoom off.   You cut precious minutes from your schedule, allowing you to get to the really good stuff someone else is peddling.

And, oh, the stuff.   How about a pair of Cat Tracks walking soles?   These are plastic treads that "prevent unsafe wear of boot soles, provide amazing comfort and pack neatly into your pocket. "   Yours for 50 cents.   Or how about an electric rock?   Or "It's a Colonel Sanders Christmas" album?   If you're a reader, "Math For Pleasure" should provide countless hours of fun.   I also discovered in "Myth Information" that more people are killed by lightning in their homes than outdoors.   Oh good.   Something more to worry about.   And all for 25 cents.

And while I'm on reading, rumor has it that the Bible is the best selling book in the world.   Well, people who put out these statistics have never been to garage sales.   By my calculations, Alvin Toffler's "Future Shock" is the best selling book of all time.   Some people even own two copies.   "Love Story" and anything by Rod McKuen are popular items, too.

Some things are required at garage sales.   They include mismatched silverware, wreaths, Christmas decorations, a typewriter, a broken TV, a Presto hot dogger and some object d'art.   The artwork is loosely defined as anything from a kid's fourth- grade drawing to a limited edition plate of L' Arc de Triomphe complete with "certificat d'authenticite. "   A velvet Elvis also counts.

But in the midst of all the entertaining items, you can find some really neat things. I bought myself a snazzy cherry bar, circa 1920s, with slots for glassware and booze, for $50. I unfold the thing and pretend I'm Bette Davis when friends come over. I bought four antique Jell-O molds for $2. I bought a cookbook I'd been looking for for 30 years – 25 cents.

And then there's that marble table with the cherubs. Oh, well. Not every decision is a great one.

I leave you with the greatest garage sale line overheard this summer. "No, I can't take $4 for it. I was going to donate it to a museum. But I will consider five."

This month's recipes, except one that came from a church potluck, come from the cookbooks garnered at garage sales. These are recipes I made some years back but lost. Now, like "Amazing Grace," they are found. (Are those bagpipes I hear? Are they for sale?)

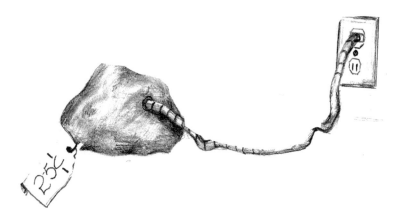

Mexican Casserole

(You'll have some canned soup left over – just mix it all together and eat it up.)

1 cup condensed cream of mushroom soup
1 cup condensed cream of chicken soup
1 cup chicken broth
1 pound cooked and diced chicken meat
1 large onion, finely chopped
1 large green pepper, finely chopped
10 corn tortillas, cut into quarters
12 ounces mixed colby and Monterey jack cheese
1 16-ounce jar hot salsa
1 14-1/2-ounce can diced tomatoes, drained

Beat soups together until creamy. In a greased 9x13-inch baking pan, layer half the ingredients, starting with the chicken. Follow with the onion, green pepper, tortillas, and cheese. Pour one cup of the soup mixture over the top and spoon on the salsa and tomatoes. Repeat. Bake at 350 degrees for 50-60 minutes. Serves 8-10.

Giant Creeping Pancake

(And I thought this one was lost forever. It's a fun dessert or snack.)

2 eggs
1/2 cup milk
4 tablespoons butter
Lemon juice

1/2 cup flour
Dash of nutmeg
Powdered sugar

Preheat oven to 425 degrees. Beat eggs. Add flour, milk and nutmeg. Melt butter in a 10- or 12-inch oven-proof skillet. Pour batter in skillet and bake for 15 minutes. Sprinkle with powdered sugar and lemon juice; bake 5 more minutes. Cut and serve. Serves 2.

Seviche

(Also known as ceviche, I would eat this appetizer by the bucketful as a teenager in Mexico. My original recipe disappeared years ago, but with the help of a garage sale cookbook I got the basics and doctored it up the way I remembered. Don't let the raw fish bother you – the lime juice "cooks" it.)

1 pound fresh sea scallops, cut into small pieces
12 tablespoons lime juice
2 large peeled and cubed tomatoes
2 green chilies, chopped
3 tablespoons olive oil
1/2 teaspoon oregano
1 teaspoon salt
Fresh ground pepper
One cup chopped fresh cilantro (the secret ingredient, a must)
1/2 small onion, sliced

Mix scallops with lime juice and refrigerate overnight.
Drain scallops and mix in remaining ingredients.
Refrigerate at least six hours to let flavors mingle.
Serves 4-8.

Cucumber
Sour Cream Mold

(Just the ticket for my antique molds with "Jell-O" imprinted on the bottoms. This is a nice, tart gelatin salad – a change from the usual sweet ones.)

1 small package lime Jell-O
3/4 cup boiling water
1/4 cup lemon juice
1 cup unpeeled cucumber, chopped
2 teaspoons diced onion
1 cup sour cream

Dissolve Jell-O in hot water. Stir in lemon juice. Chill until partially set. Stir in cucumber, onion and sour cream. Pour into a mold and chill. Serves 6.

Grasshopper Pie

(Geez, remember this one? It's so old that it's new again.)

1-1/2 cups crushed chocolate wafer crumbs
1/4 cup melted butter
3 cups miniature marshmallows
1/2 cup milk
3 tablespoons white crème de cacao
1/4 cup green crème de menthe
1-1/2 cups whipping cream
Grated chocolate

Mix crumbs with butter and press into a 9-inch pie plate. Bake at 350 degrees for 10 minutes. Cool. In top of a double boiler heat marshmallows and milk; stir until smooth. Remove from heat and stir in liqueurs. Cool. Whip cream; fold into cooled marshmallow mixture. Pour into crust and chill 3-4 hours before serving. Garnish with grated chocolate.

Grandma's Cheese Blintzes

(I know, you can buy these frozen. But they're not the same as my grandma's. These come as close to hers as I remember.)

Batter:
2 tablespoons salad oil
1 cup milk
3/4 cup flour
1/2 teaspoon salt
Butter

Filling:
1/4 pound cottage cheese
1/4 pound dry cottage cheese
2 egg yolks
2 tablespoons sugar
1 teaspoon vanilla extract

Beat eggs, oil and milk together.   Add flour and salt, beating until smooth.   Cover and chill for 30 minutes. Melt 1 teaspoon butter in a skillet.   Pour 1 tablespoon of the batter into the skillet, tipping the pan quickly so batter will cover the bottom.   Fry until light brown on one side only.   Turn out onto a plate covered with waxed paper. Stack the blintzes, browned side up and with a piece of waxed paper in between, until all the batter is used.   For the filling, beat all ingredients together until smooth. Place 1 tablespoon filling on each blintz.   Turn two opposite sides in a little and then roll up.   (You can freeze them at this time for later use.)   Fry blintzes until lightly browned on both sides.   Eat as is or top
with sour cream and/ or
a little jelly.

Jan Eshbach's
Divine Shortbread Cookies

(While these contain the same ingredients as shortbread, the texture is – well, heavenly. They're soft and powdery on the outside, buttery on the inside.)

1 cup butter
1 cup sugar
1-1/2 cups flour

Mix all ingredients together. Drop from a teaspoon onto ungreased cookie sheets. Bake at 300 degrees for 20 minutes. Keep a close eye on them so they do not brown. Makes a lot. Goes quickly.

Chicken Liver Pate

(You can easily double this recipe to have plenty on hand for a party. The crock freezes nicely.)

1/2 pound chicken livers
1 teaspoon salt
Pinch cayenne
1/2 cup softened butter
1/4 teaspoon nutmeg
1 teaspoon dry mustard
1/8 teaspoon cloves
2 tablespoons minced onions

Boil the chicken livers in water barely to cover; simmer for 15-20 minutes. Drain. Place them in a blender or food processor. Puree them. Add remaining ingredients and mix in blender or processor until well blended. Pack it into a crock and chill.

Spinach and Cheese Squares

(Yummy little nibbles at parties. They also make great breakfast squares. You can pop them in plastic bags in the freezer and pull them out to microwave in a pinch.)

4 ounces butter
3 eggs
1 cup flour
1 cup milk
1 teaspoon salt
1 teaspoon baking powder
1 pound grated Monterey Jack cheese
2 10-ounced boxes frozen spinach, thawed

Melt butter in a 9x13-inch pan. Beat eggs. Add flour, milk, salt and baking powder. Add cheese and spinach, mixing well. Spread into pan and bake at 350 degrees for 35 minutes. Cool 30 minutes before serving.
Cut into 40 squares.

HELP!

I've fallen and I can't remember to get up

Do you remember why you walked into the room? Where you put your glasses? That seven-digit phone number without looking twice? If so, you're under forty. I noticed my memory failing some years back, but ignored the signs. Sure I left the eggs out of the cake, the cats outside overnight, my keys in the back door for two days. Doesn't everyone? It was when I washed my hair with the conditioner that I faced the problem head-on. I took a Czech language class.

I read somewhere that learning a language kept you from losing your mind. Count me in. Anyone could learn Spanish, French or Italian, I figured. But Czech? Only Czechs learned Czech. Mastering that would be an experience and a challenge. My mind was ready for both.

So, I paid my money, bought the books and showed up. I thought I did well to get that far. The first lesson was great – *dobre den* (good day). I leaned that I was a *professorka* who drove an *auto*. Easy...and fun!

Then the second week arrived...and the third...and the fourth. Suddenly I didn't know a noun from a verb, a pronoun from and adjective. My eyes widened when our teacher proclaimed that we would only have to learn five cases. "Cases of what...beer?" Matching up objects, verbs, gender and other assorted item in the accusative or imperative was beyond my mental horizon.

My teacher was so cute, enthusiastic and...Czech. She talked of her hometown in the Czech Republic. We sang Czech and Slovak songs. We ate tasty Czech goodies at Christmas time. I tried to please her. I mumbled, I stumbled, I smiled. I dropped out.

But, I came back—like one of those spring-back Bozo dolls you punch. I showed up the next year with the next crop of nascent Czech students. I felt confident. I already knew how to ask "What color is that yellow wastebasket?" And "Is that an airplane hanging from your ear?" They were still on *dobre den*. Week after week I trudged to class, book and notepad under my arm, determined to conquer those cases. I thought I sounded pretty good. I talked about passports, fizzy water and coffee houses. Oh, how Bohemian! I pictured me with a Pilsner and a foot-long dark-colored cigarette at a Prague café holding court with scruffy poets, musicians and artists.

Still, I could feel it coming...the scramble to reach those words, like a kolache attached to a string someone was pulling. The jig was up the sixth week. It was my turn to ask a classmate a question. I looked at him, squared my shoulders and authoritatively inquired, "What color has been your name on the green shirt you worn tomorrow in the hatbox?" Case closed. End of lesson. . Turn in book. Memory beyond repair.

Do you smell something burning? Is that my checkbook in the dryer? Could have sworn I put it in the dishwasher.

And now, for some Czech recipes. These are from my Czech grandmother's kitchen. Dobre den, grandma.

Grandma Sintay's Nut Cookies

(These have a bazillion fat grams each.
But grandma, who had ten children, needed the energy to
shepherd the brood into adulthood.)

Dough:
4 cups flour
1 pound butter
1/2 pint sour cream

Mix together and chill overnight.

Filling:
3 cups ground walnuts
1 cup sugar
2 teaspoons cinnamon
Raisins (optional)
(If it's too dry, moisten with a little milk.)

Roll out dough and cut into circles with a glass turned
upside-down. Place a dab of filling one each one and
pinch two edges together in the middle, forming a log
that's open on one each end. Bake at 350 degrees for 20
minutes. Sprinkle with powered sugar when cool.

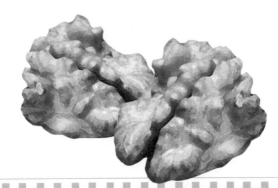

Walnut-Cinnamon Coffee Cake

(Christmas and Easter were
not complete without this cake.)

2 packages yeast
1 1/2 cups potato water
1 cup butter
1 cup cooked potato, sieved
2/3 cup sugar
1 1/2 teaspoon salt
1 teaspoon mace
2 eggs
8 cups flour

Sprinkle yeast into 1/2 cup very warm potato water (save
rest of water). Add butter to potatoes and stir until
melted. Add rest of water, sugar, salt and mace to
potatoes, mixing well. Stir in yeast.
Beat in eggs and 5 cups flour until smooth. Gradually stir
in rest of flour, making a firm dough. Knead for 10
minutes. Place in a greased bowl, turning once to grease
surgace. Cover, let rise until doubled (about another
hour.)
Divide dough in half. Roll into 18x2-inch rectangle,
about 1/2-inch thick. Spread half of the filling over
dough. (Use the same filling that's in the nut cookies.)
Roll like a jelly roll. Pinch edges and ends of dough to
seal. Place dough, seam side down, on a cookie sheet,
shaping into a horseshoe. Cover dough and let rise in
warm place until doubled (about 45 minutes).
Put dough into oven and bake at 300 degrees for 15
minutes, then turn oven to 350 degree for 30 minutes.
Turn oven to 300 degrees for 5 minutes. Turn oven off
and leave cake in for another 10 minutes. (Total baking
time is 1 hour.) Make sure cake doesn't get too dark.
If desired, sprinkle with powered sugar.

Holiday Sausage

*(My dad made this for breakfast at Christmas and Easter.
Delicious. But don't get near anyone for a week or so – the
blast of garlic will knock them over.)*

4 pounds veal, ground once
1 pound pork, ground once
2 teaspoons caraway seeds
2 tablespoons salt
1 teaspoon pepper
5 cloves garlic, crushed
1 1/2 cups cold water
Paprika for color
Casings

Mix meat ingredients thoroughly. Let meat mixture stand
for one day in refrigerator. Wash casings thoroughly. (A
good way to do it is to put them on the kitchen sink
faucet, then turn on the water and slowly pull the casings
off.) Stuff meat into casings. Refrigerate until ready to
fry.

Stuffed Green Peppers

(So good on a cold, wintry day.)

1 pound ground beef
1/3 cup uncooked rice
1 teaspoon salt
4-5 green peppers
Large can tomato juice
Pinch of sugar

Core and wash peppers. Stuff with mixture of ground beef,
uncooked rice, salt and sugar. Pour tomato juice in pan
and place peppers inside. Bring tomato juice to a boil on
top of the stove. Cover and simmer 2 hours.

Chicken and Stuffing

In large skillet, melt 4 tablespoons butter; add 1 3-pound broiler-fryer, cut up. Brown on both sides.

When chicken is browned, cover and cook over low heat for 30 minutes.

Make stuffing: In medium bowl, place 4 to 5 cups day-old Italian bread, cut into cubes. Add 1 cup milk; let soak1 hour. Mix in 1 teaspoon salt, 1/2 teaspoon black pepper, 1 teaspoon poultry seasoning, 1/2 cup fresh chopped parsley and 1 egg. Mix well.

Place chicken pieces in shallow baking dish. Spread stuffing on top of chicken. Bake, uncovered, in 375-degree oven for 30 minutes or until stuffing is golden brown. Baste with 1/4 cup melted butter from time to time. Makes 4 servings.

Rozky

Dough:
1 1/2 pounds flour
1 pound butter
1 tablespoon sugar
1 tablespoon baking powder
1 teaspoon salt
1 large can evaporated milk
4 egg yolks

Favorite filling (poppy seed, ground nuts, jam)

Mix dough ingredients together until well blended and dough doesn't stick to your hands. Refrigerate for 1 hour. Roll out on floured board and cut into squares. Put a teaspoon or so of your favorite filling on top of each square. Roll and turn into crescents. Brush tops with milk or beaten egg. Bake at 350 degrees for 30 minutes. Cool and sprinkle with powered sugar, if desired.

Chicken Soup

(A bowl of this and a glass of Vernor's magically cured all colds when I was a child.)

Soup:

3-4 pound chicken
3 parsnips
1 large onion, studded
with 3 whole cloves
1 tablespoon salt

3 carrots
2 stalks celery, with tops
1 bay leaf
1/4 teaspoon pepper

Wash chicken, cup up or leave whole. Cover with water in a 6-quart pot and bring to a boil. While boiling, keep skimming foam from top until none remains (about 5-10 minutes). More water may have to be added at this point to keep the chicken covered. Add remaining ingredients and cook gently for 1 1/2 hours, with cover tilted. Discard vegetables, remove chicken and chill broth. When soup is cold, any fat can easily be skimmed from top. Cut chicken into chunks and put into broth. Add noodles.

Noodles:

Mix three eggs together with enough flour to make a stiff dough. Knead very well on floured board until smooth and elastic. Put into bowl for about 10 minutes to rest. Roll out on lightly floured board until very thin. Let dry for a few minutes.

Now the fun begins! Cut out circles and holes by using a doughnut cutter. To make curly noodles, cut dough into strips and wind around anything small and round in the house – knitting needles, wooden spoon handles, etc. Let dry and pull off. Of course, you can make just plan old noodle-shaped noodles by cutting them into strips. But have fun and use cookie cutters or whatever else you want.

After the noodles have dried, packed them in plastic bags or store in glass jars. They're very pretty on the kitchen counter in glass containers.

To add to the soup: drop amount desired into soup. Cook over medium heat 8-10 minutes or until done.

Cheesecake

(This is an unusual cheesecake because it doesn't have any crust – crumb or otherwise.)

2 8-ounce packages cream cheese
1 pound small curd cottage cheese
4 eggs
1 1/2 cups sugar
3 tablespoons cornstarch
3 tablespoons flour
1 1/2 tablespoons lemon juice
1 teaspoon vanilla
1 pint sour cream
1/2 cup melted butter

Beat cream cheese, cottage cheese and sugar with eggs until well blended. Add cornstarch, flour, lemon juice and vanilla. Beat well. Add melted butter and sour cream, beating until smooth. Pour into greased 9-inch springform pan. Bake at 325 degrees for 1 hour, 10 minutes. Test around edges for firmness. Turn off off and let the cake remain there for 2 hours. Remove sides of pan. Cool completely for 2 hours in refrigerator.
(This cake can be frozen. It should be stored in the refrigerator.)

From Post-it notes to socks: Time to count my blessings

This Thanksgiving, I am thankful for:

—the amazing way Americans come together to help each other – and the rest of the world.

—the abundance we have in this country.   All you have to do is look around to see the abundance that needs to be lost.

—luggage with wheels.

—all the gizmos that made it necessary for some people to worry about Y2K.

—my weird uncle who spent two years preparing for Y2K. If anything ever goes wrong my heat/ water/ food supply, I will move in with him.

—living in a state that is surrounded by water. (See Y2K and uncle reference.)

—my husband.
—cotton-poly blends.
—my daughter.
—the polio vaccine.
—my brother.
—my sister.
—the U. S. postal service.   Try living in another country for a while, if you have any complaints about the system/ cost here.
—Post-it notes.
—elevators.
—ballpoint pens.
—the First Amendment.
—cheap gasoline. (See comments on postal system.)
—Ziplock bags.
—Law & Order — ba-bing, da da da da dum.
—Quality Dairy stores.
—my friends.
—maps.
—my cat.
—inexpensive socks, making darning obsolete.
—music of all sorts — okay, except rap.

—tattoos not being popular when I was in college.
—nose-rings not being popular when I was in college.
—Cherry Garcia.
—this great national holiday. No presents required.
—cruise control.
—my doctor and dentist.
—Johannes Gutenberg and movable type.
—books. (See above.)
—my job.
—e-mail . . . most of the time.
—the Separation of Powers.
—down comforters
—my dozens of cousins, who all still act like eight-year-
olds on days like Thanksgiving. Hey, let our kids be the
adults, we have a giant pillow fight going on.
—my 13-year-old car that still gets 30 miles to the gallon.
—the sun.
—can openers.
—air-conditioned movies . . . but not right now.
—my teachers . . . even Mrs. Peavey, who made me
stand in the corner during the entire fifth grade for
spilling a bottle of blue-black ink on the wooden
floor. The stain is still there.
—that turkey, tomorrow's leftover.

Recipes are just plain
wonderful eats this month.

A thanks for living in such a
plentiful country.

Cheese Things

(Well, these are things and they are made of cheese.)

2 sticks butter
2 1/3 cups shredded cheddar cheese
2 cups flour
2 cups Rice Crispies
2 dashes cayenne

Combine all ingredients and shape into balls the size of marbles. Flatten each ball in palm of hand and place on ungreased baking sheet. Bake 4-7 minutes at 475 degrees. Watch so they don't burn. Makes about 6 dozen.

Curried Pumpkin Soup

1/2 pound sliced mushrooms
1/2 cup chopped onion
2 tablespoons butter
2 tablespoons flour
1 teaspoon curry powder
2 cups chicken broth
3 cups canned pumpkin
1 12-ounce can evaporated milk
1 tablespoon honey
1/2 teaspoon salt
1/4 teaspoon pepper
1/4 teaspoon ground nutmeg

In a large pot, saute mushrooms and onion in butter until tender. Stir in the flour and curry powder until blended. Gradually add the broth. Bring to a boil. Cook, stirring constantly, for two minutes. Stir in pumpkin, milk, honey, salt, pepper and nutmeg. Serves 8.

Baked Stuffed Shrimp Casserole

(Can be used as an appetizer or main dish.)

2 pounds cleaned shrimp
3 cups soft bread crumbs
1 cup melted butter
1 cup sherry
1/2 teaspoon garlic salt
1/2 teaspoon paprika
1/4 cup parsley

Place shrimp on bottom of 11x13-inch baking dish.   Cover with bread crumbs.   Combine remaining ingredients and pour over shrimp and crumbs.   Bake for at 250 degrees for 30 minutes.   Serves 8.

Bleu Spinach Salad

(Anything with bleu cheese in it is good. Case closed.)

1 pound baby spinach leaves
1/2 pound thinly sliced mushrooms
Bleu cheese to taste, crumbled
3 slices cooked and crumbled bacon

Dressing: 2 parts olive oil to one part vinegar (so it adds up to about 1/4 - 1/3 cup total — just eyeball it)
1 teaspoon sugar
Few drops Worcestershire sauce
Dash of paprika, garlic salt, pepper and dry mustard

Mix spinach, mushrooms, cheese and bacon. Mix dressing and add at last minute. Toss. Serves 4-6.

Curried Chicken Breasts

2 whole chicken breasts
4 tablespoons butter
1/2 cup honey
1/4 mustard
2 teaspoons salt
1 tablespoon curry powder

Divide chicken breasts in half. Melt butter; stir in
remaining ingredients. Roll chicken in sauce and place
meaty side up in shallow baking pan. Pour remaining
sauce over chicken. Bake at 375 degrees for 1 hour.
Serves 2- 4, depending on how hungry you are.

Quick Oatmeal Cake

(To help you fight the winter winds — nothing will blow you down after a piece of this substantial cake.)

Cake
1 1/4 cups boiling water
1 cup quick oats
1/2 cup shortening
1 cup light brown sugar
1 cup white sugar
2 eggs
1 1/2 cups flour
1 teaspoon cinnamon
1/2 teaspoon salt
1 teaspoon baking soda

Pour boiling water over oats and let stand 20 minutes. Cream shortening and sugars. Add eggs and beat well. Add oatmeal, flour, cinnamon, salt and soda. Pour into 9x12-inch greased cake pan and bake for 20 minutes at 350 degrees. Add topping and return cake to oven for about 10 minutes longer.

Topping
6 tablespoons butter
1 cup light brown sugar
1/4 cup heavy cream
1 teaspoon vanilla
1 cup shredded coconut

Melt butter and add sugar, cream, vanilla and coconut. Spread over cake as soon as it comes from the oven.

Wild Rice and Turkey Casserole

(Had to include one recipe that will use up the leftover turkey.)

1 cup uncooked wild rice, soaked in water overnight
1 pound sliced mushrooms
1 chopped onion
6 tablespoons butter
2 teaspoons salt
1/4 teaspoon ground pepper
3 cups diced cooked turkey
1/2 cup sliced almonds
3 cups turkey or chicken broth
1 1/2 cups heavy cream
3 tablespoons grated Parmesan cheese

Cover rice with boiling water and soak for 1 hour. Drain well. Sauté mushrooms and onion in 1 tablespoon butter until onion is transparent. In buttered casserole, combine rice, vegetables, salt, pepper, turkey and almonds. Mix broth and cream; add to casserole. Cover and bake at 350 degrees for 1/2 hours. Sprinkle with cheese and dot with remaining 5 tablespoons butter. Bake at 450 degrees for 5 minutes. Serves 6.

Clean-Out-Your-Liquor Cabinet Coffee

(The title speaks for itself.)

3/4 ounces Kahlua
1/2 ounce Grand Marnier
1/4 ounce Amaretto
Coffee
Whipped cream

Pour liqueurs into a tall glass, such as an Irish coffee mug. Fill with hot coffee and top with whipped cream. Garnish with shaved chocolate. Serves 1.

Chocolate Mousse Cake

(Got to have a chocolate recipe in here.)

1 1/4 cups butter
1 1/2 cups sugar
10 ounces semi-sweet chocolate, melted and cooled
1 teaspoon instant coffee
10 eggs, separated

Cream together butter and sugar. Add chocolate and coffee; blend well. Add egg yolks one at a time and beat for 15 minutes. Beat eggs whites until stiff; fold into chocolate mixture. Refrigerate 1/4 of mixture. Pour remainder into a greased 9-inch springform pan. Bake at 350 degrees for 50 minutes. Cool completely in pan. Spread remaining chocolate mixture over top. Cover and chill overnight. Serve with slightly sweetened whipped cream. Serves 10-12.

The giant balloon drop

It's December. Never too soon to start thinking about New Year's Eve. However, I planned ahead. I did my once- in- a- lifetime celebrating a year ago when I went to the Giant Balloon Drop. This year I can stay home in my pajamas.

My New Year's Eve extraordinarie took place in Cairns, Australia, the paradise resort town in northern Queensland. I was in Australia vacationing with my daughter, Jessica, on vacation from her Peace Corps job Since I hadn't seen her for almost a year, I really didn't need any more celebration. Just being together again was quite enough excitement for me. But, being an American used to seeing the ball in Times Square and all . . . well, here's the story.

The first sign that New Year's Eve was at hand appeared when I looked up while floating in a swimming pool in time to see a firework. One lonely spray of white sparks scattered through the air, accompanied by the sound of two pops. That was the official sky burst celebration of the city of Cairns ("Let's just take life easy") Australia. It was my signal that I would have to get with it if we were to celebrate like Americans.

First stop was at an outdoor — what am I writing about, everything is outdoors when it's 90 degrees — second-story pub to view the passersby. Directly across the street a huge lighted silhouette of Batman flitted up and down an office building, although, of course, no one actually works in Cairns. On the street below, children dressed in costumes ran to the town square a block away for a party. As '60s rock 'n' roll cranked up on the loudspeakers, Jessica and I polished off our champagne cocktails. We did have an American schedule to keep.

On to an outdoor cafe for a camel, emu and kangaroo dinner. No, it didn't taste like chicken — it tasted like camel, emu and kangaroo. Really pretty good for such bizarre fare. We ordered mango ice cream for dessert and waited . . . and waited . . . and waited. Even by Cairns standards, where time is measured by how long it takes the sun to move from one palm tree to another, it was getting on. I walked inside the cafe to suggest that our waiter get on with it. I found a hapless manager alone with a pen and pad in hand. It seems the waiters had other things to do that evening and all took off. The manager raced around, loosely speaking, taking orders. He then disappeared into the kitchen. As smoke poured forth, I decided our mango ice cream was not that critical. I left a $50 bill by the cash register.

Jessica and I headed to the big event — actually the ONLY event besides the kids party — in town, the Giant Balloon Drop at the Reef Casino. We had been bombarded all week by TV ads and flyers proclaiming "Greatest Event Of The Year," "Wow," and "Big, Big, Big." We joined the throngs of people, dressed in everything from evening gowns to bikinis heading to the hotel/casino complex. Just inside the door stood a white refrigerator, the grand prize for the night.
A paper tacked to the side of the appliance listed features like ice cubes trays and vegetable bins that were part of the prize. There were no instructions as to how you could win the refrigerator — only that it was the grand prize.

We muscled our way in with 2,000 — the total population of Cairns, I think — other revelers to a small circular two-story room. This was the site of the Giant Balloon Drop. In the crush I managed to spot a sign that said something like "Capacity limited to 50 people. Order of fire marshal." Oh well. We still had about 15 minutes until midnight, so I suggested we try our luck at the "pokies," Aussie for the slots. I fished a quarter out of my purse and stuck it in. I pushed a large red button on the front of the machine. All sorts of things — skate boards, piranhas, fireballs — spun and jumped around the screen. I sat there slackjawed. What was that all about? Now what? Jessica and I looked around the machine and under the stool for directions. This game made absolutely no sense at all. A woman next to me pointed with her cigarette, "Hey, you're a winner. Keep going." She motioned for me to push the red button again. I did. Buzzards, lemon pies and airplanes flew around the screen. "Well, aren't you the lucky one," she said. "You're on a roll." "Yes," I said. "But what am I doing?" "Doesn't make a whole lot of difference, does it? You're winnin'." Hard to argue with that. I pushed the button again as she pressed her head next to mine. "I don't believe it. You won again." But now the countdown had begun. Jessica and I needed to get to the center of the room to get in on the Giant Balloon Drop. I cashed out — $5.

We elbowed our way into the pack of people. About 100 white balloons rested in a net near the ceiling. Three, two, one. Happy New Year! Down came the balloons — with a thud. A clump of balloons. The handful of people directly in the center got clobbered by balloons. Everyone cheered as the handful stomped the balloons to death. Jessica and I stared in amazement. That was it. By 12:05 the place was empty except for a roulette worker and a couple, who obviously missed the Giant Balloon Drop, romancing on a couch in the corner. On our way out I put my $5 on black at a roulette table, doubling my loot. As we neared the front door, I spotted a man in a tank top, bathing suit and flip flops carting off the refrigerator on a dolly. Hey, was that our waiter?

Back in our apartment, Jessica and I marveled at how we had actually attended a Giant Balloon Drop. We could now go to bed knowing, like the rest of Cairns, that we had not missed the greatest event of the year. Wow. Big, big, big.

As you can tell, it's pretty hard to top that New Year's Eve for entertainment. Have to wait another lifetime to do it. At least that's what I thought as I floated in the pool the following day as the people in New York were watching the clock count down to midnight. Ha! I bet no one there got a refrigerator.

Recipes are, what else, from Australia — got an extra emu on hand? Now, remember, I was there during their summer. So hang onto some of these for next June. Many of these came from a magazine called "Austalian Good Taste." Others came from our apartment manager.

Breakfast In A Glass

We drank mango smoothies made with premium ice cream at least twice a day in Australia. This recipe, I presume, is a little better for you.

1 cup milk
1 small peeled and chopped mango
1 tablespoon almond meal
2 teaspoons wheat germ
1- 2 teaspoons honey
1 passion fruit, pulp removed

Place all ingredients, except passion fruit, in a blender and blend until smooth. Stir in the passion fruit. Drink while cold.

Baked Salmon
With Lime Mayonnaise

(Okay. I know you're not supposed to eat raw eggs. But sometimes you have to take your life in your hands, particularly when it comes to good eating.)

1 2-pound deboned salmon fillet
2 large thinly sliced lemons
1 bunch dill, leaves picked
Lime or lemon wedges
Salt and pepper

Lime Mayonnaise
2 eggs yolks
Rind and juice of 2 limes
3/4 cup light olive oil
Salt and pepper

Line a large roasting pan with a piece of foil. Place 1/2 lemon slices and 1/2 the dill where salmon is to be placed. Put salmon fillet on top. Sprinkle remaining dill on top; top with remaining lemon slices. Season with salt and pepper. Bring edges of foil together and enclose the salmon. Bake at 350 degrees for 25-35 minutes — depending on thickness of fish — or until just cooked. To make the lime mayonnaise, place the egg yolks and lime juice in a blender and mix. With the blender still running, gradually add the olive oil in a very thin stream until the mixture is thick and pale. Add the lime rind; season with salt and pepper. Unwrap the salmon and remove the layer of lemons. Using two forks, carefully lift pieces of the flesh onto serving plates. Serve with the mayonnaise and lime or lemon wedges. Serves 6-8.

Garlic Herb Chicken Burgers With Tomato Mint Salad

*(Barbies [barbecues] are everywhere in Northern Australia.
The biggest amenity a hotel can offer patrons is a barbie area.)*

1/2 cup parsley leaves
1/2 cup basil leaves
1/4 cup mint leaves
1 pound chicken breasts, roughly chopped
1/4 cup milk
3 large garlic cloves, crushed
Salt and pepper
Oil
Lettuce leaves
Hamburger buns

Tomato Mint Salad
1/2 pound quartered cherry tomatoes
1/2 small finely diced red onion
1/4 cup shredded fresh mint
1/2 teaspoon sugar
Salt and pepper

Place parsley, basil and mint in a food processor. Process
in short bursts until chopped. Add chicken, milk, garlic,
salt and pepper to taste; process until chicken is finely
minced. Transfer to a bowl; cover and chill for 15
minutes. To make the salad, combine the remaining
ingredients. Cover and set aside until ready to serve.
Brush barbecue with oil to lightly grease. With wet hands,
shape the chicken mixture evenly into 4 patties. Cook on
the barbie 4-5 minutes on each side, or until cooked
through. Arrange the lettuce leaves on the bottom half of
the buns. Top with hot patties. Finish with the tomato
mint salad.

Asian Lamb Cutlets

(Lamb is a barbie favorite.)

12 lamb cutlets
1 tablespoon ground coriander

Asian Sauce
6 peeled shallots
4 large coriander roots
3 small deseeded red chilies
4 garlic cloves
1 cup lightly packed brown sugar
Juice of one lime
1 1/2 tablespoons fish sauce

Sprinkle both sides of lamb cutlets with ground coriander to lightly coat. Set aside. To make the sauce, put remaining ingredients in a food processor and process until combined. Grease the barbie. Cook cutlets 2-3 minutes each side for medium, or until cooked to your taste. Serve immediately with the sauce spooned over. Serves 4-6.

Cointreau Fruit Skewers

(Soak 8 short wooden skewers in water for about 10 minutes so they don't burn on the . . . um, barbie.)

1/2 pound strawberries, hulled and halved
3 medium sliced bananas
3 medium peaches, cut into large chunks
2 tablespoons sugar
1 tablespoon Cointreau

Thread pieces of strawberry, banana and peaches alternately onto skewers. Place skewers on a grill tray lined with foil. Sprinkle evenly with sugar. Grill 5-7 minutes or until sugar has melted and fruit starts to brown. Place on serving platter and drizzle with the Cointreau.

Barbecued Prawns

24 (2 pounds) large king prawns
1/2 teaspoon salt
1/2 teaspoon pepper
1 tablespoon olive oil

Sauce
1/2 cup extra virgin olive oil
1/3 cup chopped fresh parsley
3 garlic crushed cloves
1/2 teaspoon salt
1/2 teaspoon pepper

Place whole unpeeled prawns in a large bowl and sprinkle
with salt and pepper; mix in 1 tablespoon olive oil. Set
aside. In a small jar, shake remaining ingredients. Set
aside. Grease barbie. Add prawns and cook for 1-2
minutes on each side or until the prawns just turn pink.
Serve immediately with sauce spooned over.

Green Bean and Tomato Salad

(A change from the usual green bean recipes.)

1 pound green beans, sliced diagonally
1/4 cup olive oil
Juice and rind of 1 lemon
2 teaspoons Dijon mustard
2 crushed garlic cloves
Salt and pepper
4 medium chopped tomatoes
1/2 cup chopped parsley

Cooks beans in boiling water for 2 minutes. Drain and
rinse under cold water. Drain; place in serving bowl. In a
small jar, shake the olive oil, lemon rind, juice, mustard,
garlic and salt and pepper. Add the dressing, tomatoes and
parsley to the beans. Toss well to combine.

Chocolate Pudding Cake

(Yes, we did our share of chocolate-eating.)

1/2 cup firmly packed brown sugar
1 cup self-rising flour
2 tablespoons cocoa powder
3/4 cup thin cream
2 1/2 tablespoons melted butter
Powdered sugar
Whipped cream

Sauce
3/4 cup firmly packed brown sugar
2 tablespoons cocoa powder
1 1/2 cups boiling water

Grease a 6-cup microwave-safe dish with butter. Place sugar in a medium mixing bowl. Sift flour and cocoa over the sugar. Stir to combine. Stir in the cream and butter, mixing into a smooth batter. Spoon into the greased dish. To make the sauce, combine the brown sugar and cocoa in a bowl. Sprinkle evenly over batter. Pour the boiling water in a steady stream over the back of a large metal spoon evenly over the batter. Microwave, uncovered, for 13-15 minutes on medium. The center may be undercooked, but will continue cooking on standing. Cover loosely with foil and let stand for 5-10 minutes. Dust with powdered sugar. Serve with whipped cream. Serves 4-6.

Recipe Index

This & That

Breads

Salads
and Vegetables

Soups

Main Dishes

Desserts

For information on other Eberly Press books, write to:

Eberly Press

403 Frankfort Avenue
Elberta, Michigan 49628
michigancooking.com